Weeds of the Woods

WEEDS
of the
WOODS

*small trees and shrubs
of the eastern forest*

GLEN BLOUIN

NIMBUS
PUBLISHING

Copyright © Glen Blouin, 1992, 2004

All rights reserved. No part of this book may be reproduced, stored in a retrieval system or transmitted in any form or by any means without the prior written permission from the publisher, or, in the case of photocopying or other reprographic copying, permission from Access Copyright, 1 Yonge Street, Suite 1900, Toronto, Ontario M5E 1E5.

Nimbus Publishing Limited
PO Box 9166
Halifax, NS   B3K 5M8
(902) 455-4286

Cover design: Kathy Kaulbach, Paragon Design Group

Printed and bound in Canada

Library and Archives Canada Cataloguing in Publication

Blouin, Glen
Weeds of the woods : small trees and shrubs of the eastern forest / Glen Blouin.

Reprint. First published 1992.
ISBN 1-55109-504-1

1. Trees—Canada, Eastern. 2. Trees—East (U.S.) 3. Shrubs—Canada, Eastern. 4. Shrubs—East (U.S.) I. Title.

QK203.M37B56 2004   582.16'09715   C2004-904179-7

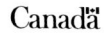

We acknowledge the financial support of the Government of Canada through the Book Publishing Industry Development Program (BPIDP) and the Canada Council for our publishing activities.

To Stéphanie and Phillip

CONTENTS

Introduction	ix
Speckled Alder	14
Mountain Ash	20
Staghorn Sumac	24
Red Osier Dogwood	28
Alternate Leaf Dogwood	34
Beaked Hazelnut	38
Striped Maple	42
Mountain Maple	46
Elderberry	50
Red Berried Elder	56
Pin Cherry	60
Choke Cherry	66
Hawthorn	70
Canada Yew	76
Serviceberry	80
Witch Hazel	86
Willow	92
Hobblebush	98
High Bush Cranberry	102
Wild Raisin	108
Quotation Sources	115
Glossary	116
Bibliography — Books	118
Bibliography — Periodicals	121

INTRODUCTION

It is virtually impossible to live in Atlantic Canada and not know something about forests. In New Brunswick, for example, ninety percent of the province's land mass is covered by trees. One of every seven working persons is involved in harvesting trees, processing wood into finished or semi-finished products, or providing services to the forest industry. But the importance of forests goes far beyond their economic value.

Forests provide food and shelter to many species of birds and animals. Forest cover regulates the water table and helps maintain stream conditions needed by a wide variety of fish species. To many residents of eastern Canada, the recreational opportunities provided by forests are as important as the economic impact of forests on their lives.

Despite the fact that we live with forests all around us, many people have only a vague idea of the complexity of a forest ecosystem. Woody plants, flowers, ferns, fungi, grasses, insects, birds, animals, fish and people all have a role to play in the shaping of our forests.

Almost all of the eastern forest is productive, which means that it is capable of growing products that can be commercially harvested. But of the two hundred species native to the eastern forest, only a very few — mainly the spruces and balsam fir — are harvested for commercial use. The vast majority of the woody species found in a forest are small trees and shrubs that have no commercial value and are often treated as weeds.

The species that the logger sees as weeds of the woods do, however, play a vital role in the forest. They prevent soil erosion and provide the conditions needed for the seedlings of the larger tree species to get established. They provide food and shelter for wildlife. Some species take nitrogen from the air and fertilize the soil. And all of them produce oxygen which is just as fresh and breathable as that of the noblest oak.

The twenty species or groups of species described in this book were selected to provide a broad cross-section of some of the most common shrubs in the eastern forest. The selection includes a few scarce species like the witch hazel, which is included because of its intriguing flowering habits and its widespread use as a medicine. However, a number of common shrub species, like the raspberry, rhodora and winterberry, are not represented.

The three mountain ashes are treated as a group because there are only minor differences between the species. Willows, of which there are twenty-eight different species in eastern Canada, are also grouped as one. Hawthorns and serviceberries are dealt with as groups, partly because even botanists can't agree on how many separate species of these plants there are.

This book is designed to assist readers in the field identification of the various species of shrubs at different times of the year. Leaf shape, trunk and bark characteristics, flower, fruit and winter twigs are all described in detail, and, in most cases, full-color photographs of their distinctive characteristics are provided. It is hoped that the combined text and illustrations will make identification of the shrubs a simple task, even for the novice naturalist. In addition, common and local names for all species are given in French and English, Micmac and Maliseet.* To avoid any possibility of confusion, the universal scientific (Latin) name has also been provided.

For each species of shrub, information has also been included to help the reader understand the species' significance in the forest ecosystem. This information is divided into sections on habitat, value to wildlife, ornamental use, medicinal properties, edibility and other uses.

habitat . . .

The location of a shrub is often a key to its identity. A shrub's habitat for example provides clues to its role in the ecosystem, its relationship with other plant species and the range of soils where the species might be found growing.

wildlife . . .

Flowering shrubs are an important source of pollen and nectar for bees and other insects. The ripe fruit in the summer and fall are a mainstay in the diet of many species of songbirds. In winter, twigs from the shrubs are an important source of vitamins, minerals, carbohydrates and protein for browsing animals like moose or deer and for some gamebirds. Shrubs also provide shelter and nesting cover for many species of birds and small animals. Across North America, there are 181 species of birds that rely on shrubs for cover.

as an ornamental . . .

The many varieties of native shrubs are an inexpensive alternative to imported or exotic shrubs. Species such as the staghorn sumac, elderberry and mountain ash rival the exotics and imports in their aesthetic appeal. Native shrubs have the added advantage of being hardy and well adapted to the climatic extremes of eastern Canada. A few suggestions on the use of the various native shrubs for landscaping are included in this book.

---

*The author would like to thank Mildred Milliea, of the Big Cove Micmacs, and the late Peter Paul, of the Woodstock Maliseets, for verifying and correcting the Indian names.

as a medicinal . . .

The list of medicinal remedies, drugs and potions derived from wild plants is a long one. Digitalis from foxglove, aspirin from willow bark, quinine from cinchona, and, lately, a potential cancer remedy from the yew are just a few of the most notable. The medicinal potential of many other species of wild plants has never been fully explored.

In North America, Indian peoples were the first to use native plants for medicinal purposes. They knew the value of Vitamin C found in many fruits and berries, and used this knowledge to help early European explorers treat scurvy. In 1535, for example, Jacques Cartier's crew was saved from scurvy when Algonquian Indians told them to eat wild fruits rich in Vitamin C.

However, the various remedies described in this book have been presented solely for their historical value, and for the sake of curiosity. *None of the remedies is recommended*; in the wild, there are plants that can feed you or drug you, cure you or kill you!

edibility . . .

Most of the shrubs described in this book bear edible fruit. The taste of the fruit ranges from the rather bland elderberry to the pungent choke cherry. Those fruits that are not edible are clearly identified.

All the edible fruits may be used to produce jams, jellies, preserves, juices, wines and pies. A few recipes have been provided to indicate some of the possibilities.

other uses . . .

New Brunswick's native peoples and early European settlers used shrubs for a wide variety of products. Dyes were made from roots and bark. People smoked dried leaves of some shrubs. The wood was used for whittling or carving. Twigs were turned into pipe stems or spiles for tapping maple trees. Shrubs were even the source of divining rods for locating wells.

I hope this book will stimulate the interest of casual observers of nature, help broaden the perspective of forestry professionals and provide a source of reference material to students.

Most of all, I hope this book helps everyone appreciate the importance and significance of small trees and shrubs of the eastern forest, the weeds of the woods.

* * * * *

Since this book was written nine years ago, a few things have changed. As Canadians we are all more concerned about the environment. Terms like "biodiversity" are now in common usage, whether or not we know what they mean. Old growth forests are of great concern (although I have not yet heard of anyone wishing to preserve old growth alders). Clearcutting has come under close scrutiny, and the forest industry is taking steps to become more "environmentally friendly." There is heated debate about herbicides, chemicals which are sometimes used to suppress or kill many of the species described in this book.

As with the human body, we have a lot to learn about the forests, and all of the species which inhabit the forest. It's unlikely we will ever know all there is to know — that's the beauty and the mystery of nature. It is far more complex than either we or our computers can comprehend. The interaction of the various species — trees, shrubs, wildflowers, mosses, lichens, ferns, worms, micro-organisms, insects, birds and mammals — with one another and with humans forms what we call "ecosystems." The permutations and combinations are not yet fully understood and in all likelihood never will be.

A healthy respect for both what we know and do not know would be prudent. Nature is resilient. It bounces back after severe change, as evidenced in the aftermath of forest fires, clearcutting, insect epidemics or the abandonment of farms that were once forests. Somehow in the eastern forest they all bounce back. But this doesn't mean we should throw caution to the wind. The tolerance level of nature may be more finite than we assume.

Humility in trying to manage nature, in understanding how to work with nature, is necessary. Otherwise we may do irreparable harm to nature's ecosystems and, in so doing, seriously impact on our own ability to survive — economically and environmentally. Today we call this sustainable development.

Things have changed in the last nine years. But the message is the same.

* * * * *

I would like to thank Tom McKegney, Peter Pearce, Harold Hinds and Michelle LaBarre-Blouin for reviewing the material prior to publication; George Stevens, Joakim Hermelin, Margaret Carr, Dan Murphy, Rod Carrow, and Dave Baardsen for facilitating things administratively; Ken MacPherson, Paul Boucher, Eszter Schwenke, Pat Allen, Alex Dickson, Mildred and Willie John Milliea, Jane Veach, the late Peter Paul, Jocelyne

Gauvin, Margie Luffman, Ron Rouselle, Francois Blanchard, Georgina Larocque, William and Irene Simon, Francis Wihbey, Jean Bohne, Ted Bedard, Rudy Stocek, Howard Berry, Serge Morin, John Torunski and Jim Crowe for going out of their way to gather information; the staff of the New Brunswick Museum Library and Archives, the University of New Brunswick Science Library, the University of Toronto Forestry Library, the University of Toronto Science-Medicine Library and the University of Toronto Library of Botany for assistance in research; Betty Barker for typing the manuscript; and the staff of the Forest Extension Service of the New Brunswick Department of Natural Resources and Energy for their patience and cooperation.

Glen Blouin

Author's Notes to the Third Edition

A number of references to New Brunswick appear in this book. The reason is simple. It was originally published by the province's Department of Natural Resources in 1984 to celebrate the bicentennial. But trees and shrubs know no political boundaries. A choke cherry is a choke cherry, whether it grows in Nova Scotia or North Dakota. Information on each species applies throughout its range in North America.

The historical and botanical information may be timeless, but native terminology has evolved. In revisiting their roots, Micmacs have reverted to the original "Mi'kmaq," and Maliseet is now "Malisete." Similarly, terms such as "Indian" and "tribe" to describe First Nations or Native Americans may no longer be considered appropriate. They are included here as they were in the original 1984 edition. No disrespect is intended to the people who, historical records indicate, shared their traditional medicinal knowledge with European settlers, in the real sense of Christianity.

The only major change is in the chapter on Canada yew (ground hemlock). Previous editions described the success of a man relieving his multiple sclerosis symptoms with ground hemlock tea. When originally interviewed, he had misidentified the species—only later he found it was ground juniper (*Juniperus communis*). An easy mistake—both are short sprawling evergreen shrubs that bear berries. That reference has been dropped.

In its place is the recent discovery of the medicinal properties of ground hemlock. After years of experimentation and clinical trials, its extract— paclitaxel—is now routinely used in chemotherapy to treat ovarian and other forms of cancer.

Finally, I must reiterate a point made in the original introduction. None of these remedies should be tried without consulting a medical practitioner. Particularly today when severe allergies are commonplace. What could be curative, or at least harmless, to one individual might prove fatal to another.

I hope you enjoy this slightly revised third edition, take it with you into the forest, and learn a little more about our so-called "Weeds of the Woods."

Glen Blouin

common alder   aulne rugueux   Micmac: *topsi*
tag alder   vergne   Maliseet: *top*
hazel alder   varne

SPECKLED ALDER
(Alnus rugosa)

Two species of alder are native to Atlantic Canada, the most common of which is the speckled alder (Alnus rugosa). For the sake of convenience both species are considered as one.

Leaf:
The alternate, oval-shaped leaves are thick and coarsely textured. The upper side is dull, dark green with conspicuous recessed veins; the underside is pale, grey-green with raised veins. Leaf edges are uneven and sharply toothed.

Stem:
Clumps of bow-shaped stems spread laterally from the base and then upward to a maximum height of six meters. Mature alders may reach 10 cm diameter at the base, but quickly taper, fork or branch to a smaller size. The grey bark is dotted with beige lenticels. The exposed surface of freshly cut stumps turns orange.

Flower:
Burgundy-brown male catkins up to five centimetres long form in the fall. They hang from the ends of twigs in small bunches until spring. At that time they release pollen which fertilizes the smaller (one centimetre) female catkins, which are usually further in on the same twig.

Fruit:
Female catkins develop into oval, dark brown cones, similar to those of some evergreens. Once the winged seeds are released to the wind in autumn, the small (two centimetres long) cones may remain on the branches for a year or more.

Twig:
Slender, greyish brown twigs are spotted with beige lenticels and bear alternate stalked buds. The dull purplish-grey buds are approximately one centimetre long with rounded tips. The pith is dark brown and roughly triangular in cross section.

Profusion of alder catkins.

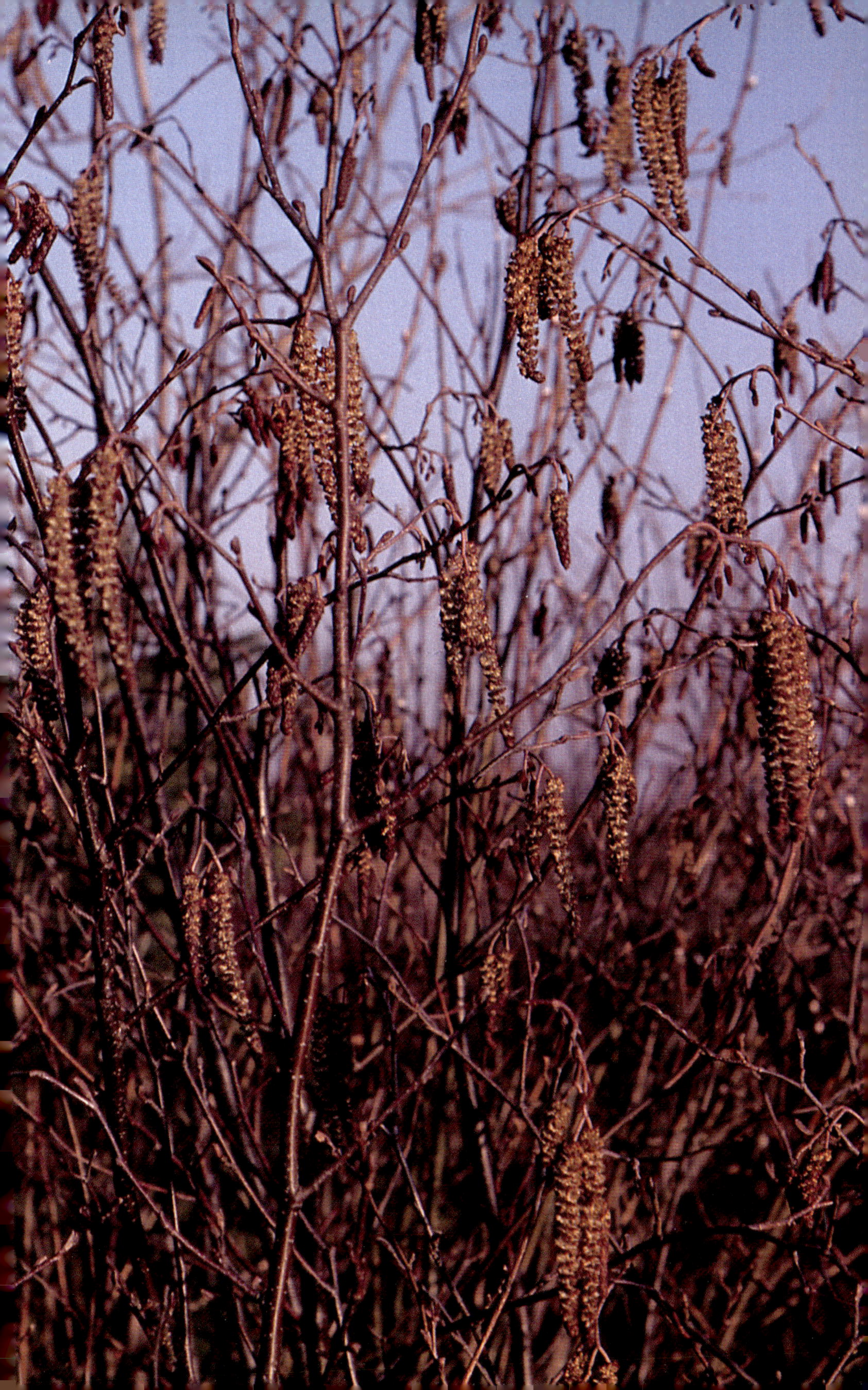

alder . . .

The profusion of alder in rural New Brunswick reflects a significant aspect of the modern history of the province. The abandoning of farm land in the 1950s and 1960s created ideal conditions for the perpetuation and spread of alders.

Alders are pioneers. They are one of the first species to invade abandoned fields, particularly those that are poorly drained. In all areas of the province, but most particularly on the east coast lowlands, thousands of hectares of once-productive farm land have been overrun by the prolific shrub.

As pioneers, alders are the first step in the natural transition of farm land back to forest. Longer-lived species such as white spruce may be suppressed in the shade of an alder thicket. But in time spruce will poke their leaders through the dense canopy of alder leaves, and that will spell the beginning of the end for the alders which cannot survive in the shade.

The alder serves yet another role in nature's plan. Alders are nitrogen fixers. Atmospheric nitrogen is absorbed by bacteria living in nodules on the alder roots and changed into a form of nitrogen plants can utilize as fertilizer. In this way alders help fertilize fields which may have been depleted of nitrogen by years of farming.

Nitrogen-fixing nodules on alder roots.

Alder leaves are also unusually rich in nitrogen. The annual deposit of leaves provides a second source of this vital element to the soil. It has been calculated that a field of alders, through the process of nitrogen fixation and annual leaf fall, can add up to 160 kg of nitrogen per hectare (140 pounds/acre) per year to the soil.

In several parts of the world, alders have been planted to fertilize plantations of larger, more valuable trees. In a Dutch experiment it was found that alders in an apple orchard raised the fruit yield by 36 per cent. In southern Ontario, alders have been interplanted with hybrid poplar to give a boost to the fast-growing poplars.

State governments in several coal-mining countries in the United States have planted alders on coal spoils to check erosion, increase fertility and build up an organic layer of soil. Alders have the potential to be to silviculture what the legumes are to agriculture.

Rough-textured leaves are somewhat irregular in shape.

as an ornamental . . .

To most people planting alders as ornamentals would be equivalent to planting dandelions on the front lawn. Alders are generally relegated to the nuisance category, along with budworm, black flies and porcupines.

Although basically unattractive, they are very hardy and resistant to insects and disease. They have some uses, usually where aesthetics are not the prime consideration, such as in windbreaks, in preventing erosion, or building up depleted soils.

wildlife . . .

Alder seeds, like those of its cousins the birches, are a winter favourite of siskins, goldfinches and redpolls. The buds are also nibbled by ruffed grouse. Beaver eat the bark and use the stems for dam and lodge construction, particularly where there is a scarcity of poplar. Moose and snowshoe hares will eat alder leaves, but they are not ranked high on their preferred list of foods.

Alders are most important to the American woodcock, which nest and rear their young under cover of alder bushes. Earthworms commonly found in the nitrogen-rich soil under an alder thicket are the diet staple of woodcock.

Large stands of alder may be managed to encourage a woodcock population by cutting in a checkerboard pattern. Clear-cutting small patches ($1/_{10}$ hectare or $1/_4$ acre) every four or five years will provide the gamebirds with the variety of clearings and cover they need for survival.

Alders bear both male and female flowers on the same branch.

as a medicinal . . .

Alders were one of the most popular medicinal shrubs of the New Brunswick Indians. The astringent properties of the bark were put to use both internally and externally. Maliseets drank bark teas to stop cramps and retching, while the Micmacs prescribed the tea to combat diphtheria. Pieces of branches or stems were boiled until the bark came off, chewed and swallowed for relief of hemorrhages of the lungs, and to promote rapid healing from wounds, fractures and dislocations. Poultices of the boiled bark were applied to cuts and bruises.

A person suffering from festers or severe fever would be wrapped in alder leaves: it was claimed that the sufferer would be cured by the time the leaves withered.

The Acadians also made good medicinal use of alder. They brewed an all-purpose tonic by boiling the bark until the water turned reddish-brown. They would drink a small glass of the liquid every day to prevent anemia and problems with the kidneys, to purify the blood, and to ward off skin diseases and boils. Some claimed that adding a little gin to the tonic would fight off jaundice.

other uses . . .

Rural residents have long been aware of the heating value of alders, particularly for a quick hot fire in the kitchen stove. Alders were at one time also extensively used in local charcoal manufacturing industries.

With the development of modern chip burning furnaces and gasifiers, there is increased potential for growing alders on a mini-rotation basis to satisfy domestic and industrial energy needs. If mowed every three to five years, alders have the potential to resprout indefinitely.

A series of studies undertaken at the University of Maine in the 1960s concluded that it is technically possible to produce Kraft pulp from weed species such as alder. Yields were as good or better than those of the more commonly used hardwood species. Alder chips or particles could also be used in the manufacture of chipboard and other building products.

Alders perform well on poorly-drained, often marginal farm land.

Alder stems in familiar clumps.

They sprout prolifically after cutting. They are relatively insect and disease free, and are self-fertilizing. There exists the potential to convert this weed of the woods into a commercially valuable crop.

removal . . .

One of the most common inquiries from woodlot owners is: "What is the best way to get rid of alders?" The alternatives are many and varied.

Pasturing goats or pigs in an alder patch has proven effective, and in the process the site is fertilized with manure. Pigs uproot the bushes, while goats will eat all the leaves within reach.

Mechanical methods of removal are perhaps more common. When the soil is dry, bulldozing with a root rake is effective if care is taken not to remove the top soil. Clearing saws and chain saws get the job done but leave stumps which will inevitably sprout the following year. This treatement must be followed up with application of a herbicide, usually mixed with fuel oil, to freshly cut stumps.

Common folk lore has it that cutting alders in "the black moon of August" will ensure that there will be no sprouting the following summer.

rowan tree
dogberry
roundwood

sorbier
cormier
maska
maskouabina

Micmac: epsemosi
Maliseet: mi-na-kwim-os

MOUNTAIN ASH
(Sorbus spp.)

Three species of mountain ash grow in New Brunswick. Two are native and the other was introduced from Europe. The American, Showy and European Mountain Ashes are generally similar in appearance and have been grouped together for the sake of simplicity.

Leaf:
Leaves are compound, each leaf actually being a composite of many small sawtoothed leaflets. There are usually 11 to 17 leaflets positioned in pairs along the stalk, with one slightly wider leaflet at the end (terminal).

Stem:
The smooth, thin, grey-green bark is dotted with sporadic whitish ovals (lenticels). At maturity, stem diameters range from 10 to 20 cm and the average height is 7 to 10 metres. The heartwood (in the centre) is pale brown, and the sapwood (the living wood around it) is white. The wood is weak, soft and light.

Flower:
Clusters of creamy-white flowers bloom at the ends of the twigs after leaves have reached full size, usually in June. Each small (approx. 1 cm across) five-petalled flower contains both male and female parts and can pollinate itself.

Fruit:
By August the flowers have evolved into bright scarlet or orange-red berries the size of peas. These may hang in clusters from the ends of branches well into winter. Each berry contains from two to ten tiny brown seeds.

Twig:
The reddish-brown twigs are smooth and rather stout. Side or lateral buds are pressed against the twig; the long terminal bud is dark, shiny, and gummy.

The mountain ashes make handsome ornamentals.

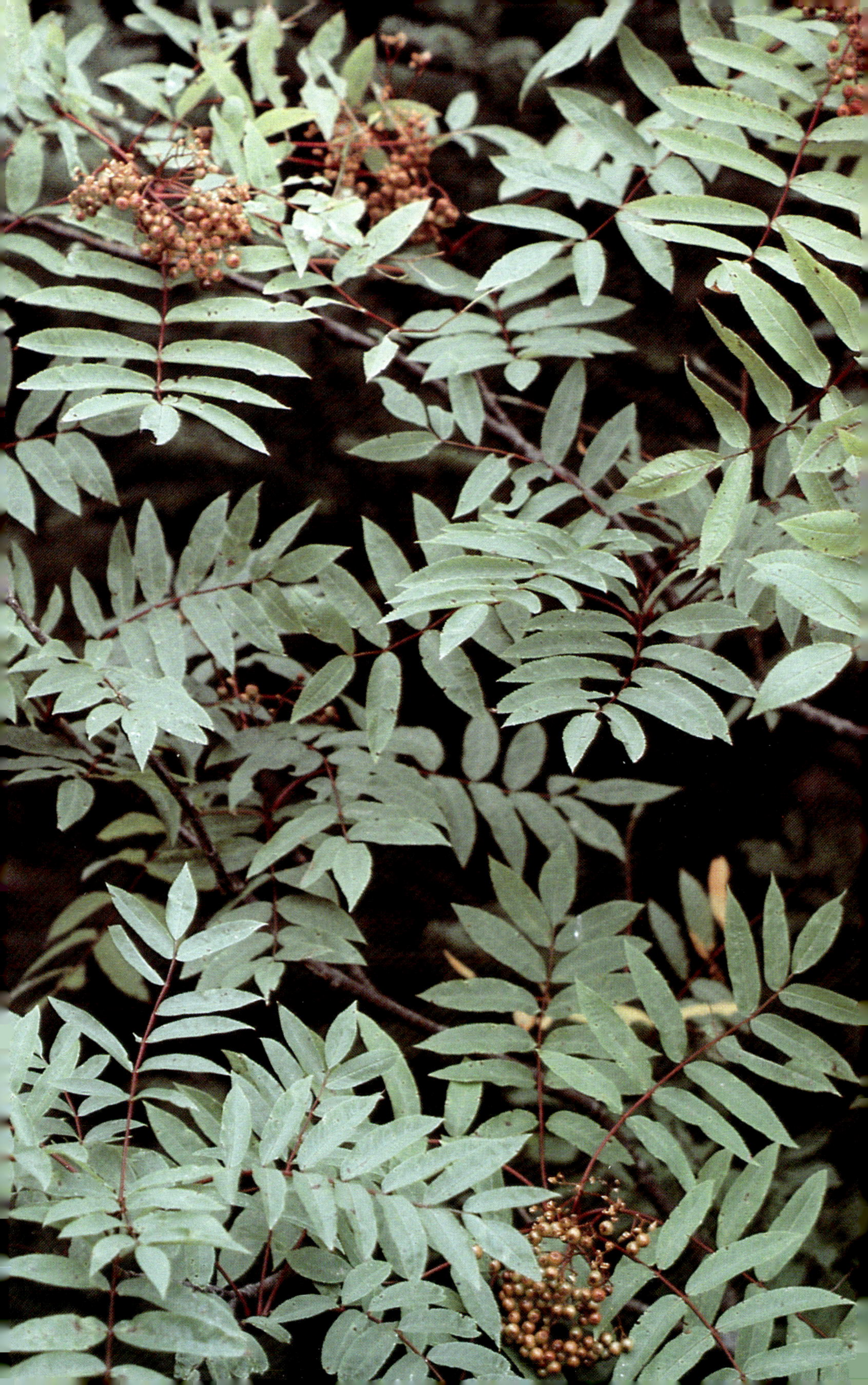

more on mountain ash . . .

Despite their name, mountain ashes are not true members of the ash family. They belong to the rose family which also includes apples, peaches, cherries, hawthorn and of course the many varieties of roses.

European mountain ash is the Rowan tree often referred to in the romantic literature of England.

as an ornamental . . .

The mountain ashes are among the most beautiful of our native trees and shrubs. The delicate foliage, showy clusters of creamy white flowers, and striking bunches of orange or scarlet berries are an ornamental delight throughout the summer.

However, they are susceptible to a number of leaf-eating insects, including the voracious tent caterpillar and the mountain ash sawfly, and may require some form of protection when these insects are abundant.

To start mountain ash from seed, gather the berries in late September and spread them out in the sun to dry. Remove the pulpy flesh and sow the tiny seeds, covering very lightly with soil.

wildlife . . .

There may be stiff competition for the berries. Many species of songbirds, including cedar waxwings, grosbeaks and robins feast on the bitter fruit. They are also a favourite of both black bears and ruffed grouse. Beaver nibble

Colourful fruit clusters attract hungry songbirds.

on the bark, and deer, moose and hares browse the winter twigs.

as a medicinal . . .

The leaves of the mountain ash contain cyanide compounds and are **poisonous.** They were frequently consumed by Maritime Indians to induce vomiting.

Raw bark was chewed by the Micmacs to alleviate pains in the stomach. The Maliseets applied poultices of the burnt bark to boils. Bark teas were used for nausea and to relieve the pain of childbirth. Solutions made from the bark were used for diarrhoea and vaginal infections.

The berries are rich in both iron and vitamin C and were used, both fresh and in teas, to treat scurvy. Prior to ripening, the fruit is high in tartaric acid and is unpalatable. After a few frosts the taste mellows and, though still bitter, the fruit becomes edible.

mountain ash berry jelly . . .

Wash ripe berries, stem, and cover with water. Boil until soft. Mash and strain through jelly bag. Boil 25 minutes. Add 1 cup sugar to each cup of juice, stirring while adding. Boil to jelly stage. Skim, seal in hot sterilized jars.

courtesy of
Alberta Dept. of Agriculture

Showy clusters of flowers appear in June.

sumach *sumac vinaigrier* Micmac: *giitaganmosi*
hairy sumac *vinaigrier* Maliseet: *sul-on-im-os*
velvet sumac

STAGHORN SUMAC
(Rhus typhina)

Leaf:
Fernlike leaves are compound. Five to fifteen pairs of dark green pointed leaflets with saw-toothed edges are arranged along stout hairy stalks, with a single, slightly wider leaflet at the end (terminal). Foliage turns a brilliant scarlet in autumn.

Stem:
The main stem, rarely over 10 cm in diameter, is usually crooked and forked. The bark is smooth and dark brown. The wood is yellowish-green and the centre (pith) is orange. Average height is about four metres.

Flower:
Large cone-shaped clusters of tiny yellowish-green flowers appear late in June. Male and female flowers are usually borne on separate shrubs.

Fruit:
At the ends of the branches, clusters of female flowers develop into dense erect clusters of crimson hairy berries (often mistakenly called flowers), which remain on the shrub throughout winter. Each little berry contains one hard flat seed.

Twig:
Winter twigs are thick, grey-brown, and covered with velvety hairs. If broken, they exude a sticky milky sap. If the outer layer of bark is peeled off, the inside is reddish-brown, the wood celery-green and the pith yellowish-brown. Buds are brown and hairy, and there is no terminal bud at the end of the twig.

A thicket of staghorn sumac in early spring.

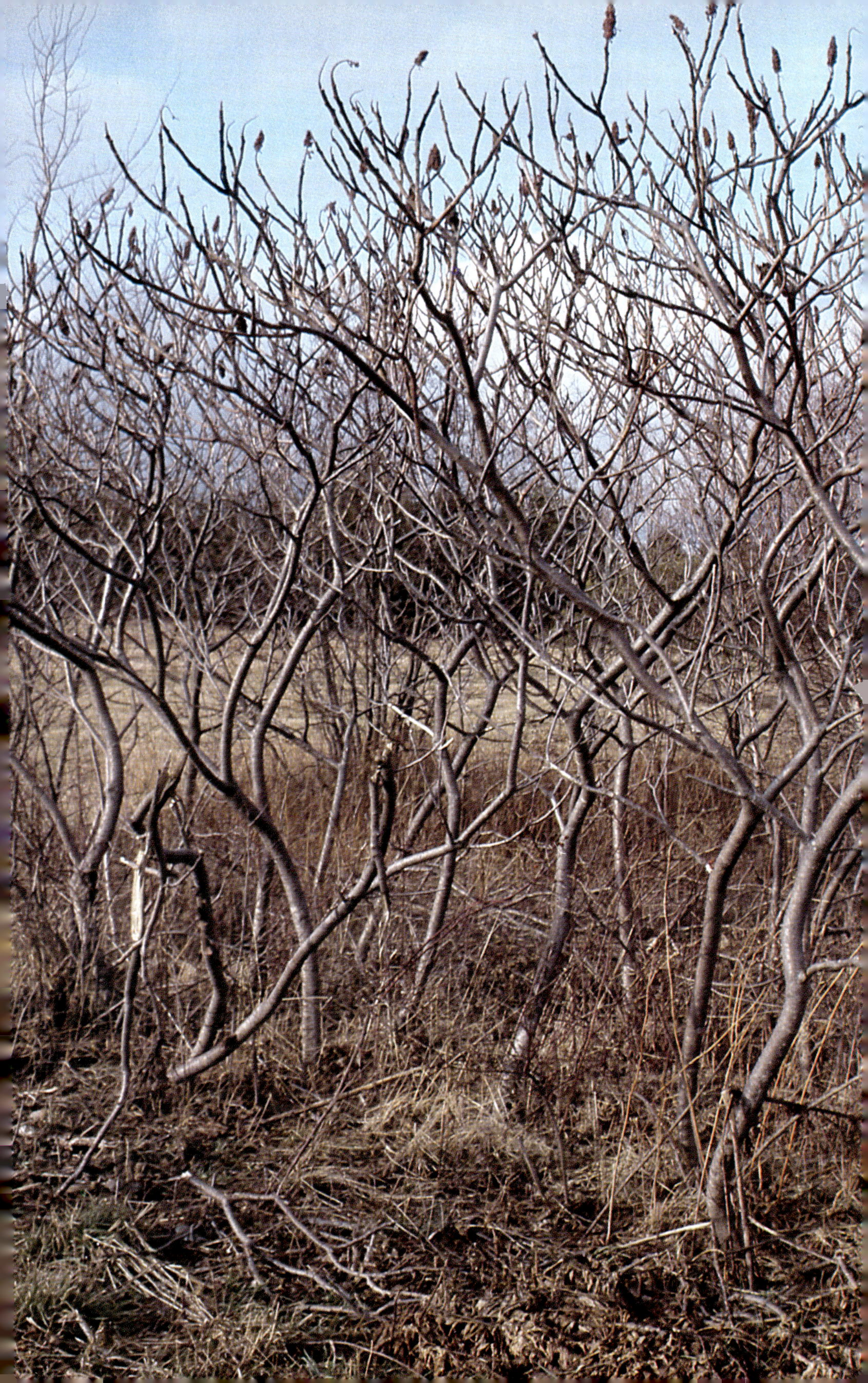

the story of sumac...

A member of the cashew family, staghorn sumac is related to the pistachio and the mango of more southern climates, and here in Canada has the dubious distinction of being first cousin to the dreaded poison ivy. It is commonly found growing on abandoned farm sites, particularly on dry gravelly or sandy, often infertile, soils.

as an ornamental...

The shallow but wide-spreading root system of the sumac makes it a natural for soil conservation and landscaping, where erosion is a problem. As a bonus, the staghorn serves as an attractive ornamental year-round. The lush green, almost tropical foliage of summer turns a brilliant red in autumn. After leaf fall, the distinctive crimson fruit clusters adorn the velvety branch tips until April or May, providing a dash of colourful relief to the browns, greys, and whites of winter.

The seed of the sumac is extremely hard — in fact partridge use it for grit — so prior to planting, seeds must be soaked in sulphuric acid for three to four hours. Seed should be sown in early spring, at a depth of 2 or 3 cm and preferably on tilled soil. In most cases it is simpler to dig up young trees from the wild and transplant them. Once planted, sumac requires little care or maintenance.

Within four or five years from planting, clones may start shooting up or "suckering" from the roots, as far away as five metres from the parent tree, eventually forming a small thicket. It is therefore not recommended that sumac be planted where space is a limiting factor, or where only one tree is desired.

wildlife...

On old fields, staghorn sumac is

Fernlike compound leaves make sumac an attractive summer ornamental.

often a key component in the diet of the ruffed grouse (partridge), as well as an important winter food of the white-tailed deer. But the primary value of the sumac to wildlife is as food for songbirds. A 1934 report cited ninety-three different species of birds eating sumac berries. It is not all that uncommon for a flock of grosbeaks to descend on a sumac thicket when food is scarce in midwinter for a feed of the hairy red berries.

other uses...

Sumac leaves are rich in tannic acid (up to thirty-five percent dry weight). In days gone by they were gathered and sold to tanneries for the production of a light-coloured Moroccan leather. Berries, leaves and roots were used for a variety of natural dyes, ranging from yellow to red to black. The orange-coloured wood is still used today by craftsmen for novelty items.

as a medicinal . . .

Sumac fruit boiled in water was widely used by Indians and pioneers alike as a gargle cure for sore throats. Decoctions from leaves and seeds were used externally and internally to shrink hemorrhoids. The steeped bark was applied for a variety of skin diseases and rashes, and to stop bleeding (astringent). Sumac has also had some experimental success as an anti-diabetes drug.

In 1830, naturalist C.S. Rafinesque made these observations:

"Berries used in dysentery, rheumatism, dysuria, sorethroat, putrid fevers, hemorrhage, gangrene & c. . . Roots antisyphilitic, leaves good astringent for all fluxes. Bark and berries make ink. Fresh roots used for rheumatism, spirituous infusion rubbed with flannel. Gum cures toothache put in hollow teeth. Indian flutes made of the stems."

recipe . . .

For a refreshing drink rich in vitamin A, gather berries as soon as mature (red) in early fall, crush lightly, and cover with boiling water. Immediately remove from heat and steep until water turns the color of pink lemonade. Strain through cheesecloth to remove seeds, pulp and hairs, sweeten with maple syrup or honey to taste, chill and serve. Like apples and grapes, sumac fruit is rich in malic acid, and makes excellent jellies, alone or in combination with other fruits.

Clusters of hairy red berries remain on twigs throughout winter.

red willow
cornel   *hart rouge*   Micmac: *spiipaganmosi*
kinnikinnik   *bois de calumet*   Maliseet: *nes-pi-tum-umk*
squawbush   *cornouiller stolonifère*

RED OSIER DOGWOOD
(Cornus stolonifera)

Leaf:
The smooth-edged (untoothed) leaves are arranged in pairs on opposite sides of the twigs. They are dark green on top, lighter underneath, and slightly fuzzy on both surfaces. As with all dogwoods, the leaves feature five to seven pairs of prominent veins which follow the shape of the whole leaf.

Stem:
Many spreading stems, the tallest of which seldom reach three metres, give the red osier dogwood a "bushy" appearance. The bark is lime-green in summer, turning wine-red in winter. It is smooth but becomes grey and coarse with age, particularly at the base. The wood is hard and heavy, but rarely reaches a commercially valuable size.

Flower:
Small (five cm) flat-topped clusters of creamy white blossoms appear at the tips of branches in June. Each tiny (six to eight cm) bisexual flower has four petals. Red osier dogwood has been known to blossom again in late summer.

Fruit:
Maturing in September, the berries are white or bluish-tinged. The flesh is edible but mealy. Each hard oval stone contains two seeds.

Twig:
The smooth red winter twigs become even brighter red in April just before the buds swell and leaves appear. When freshly cut, they exude a scent not unlike watermelon. Twigs are dotted with white oval markings (lenticels), and the small buds have a dense hairy covering.

Wine-red stems become greyer and coarser with age.

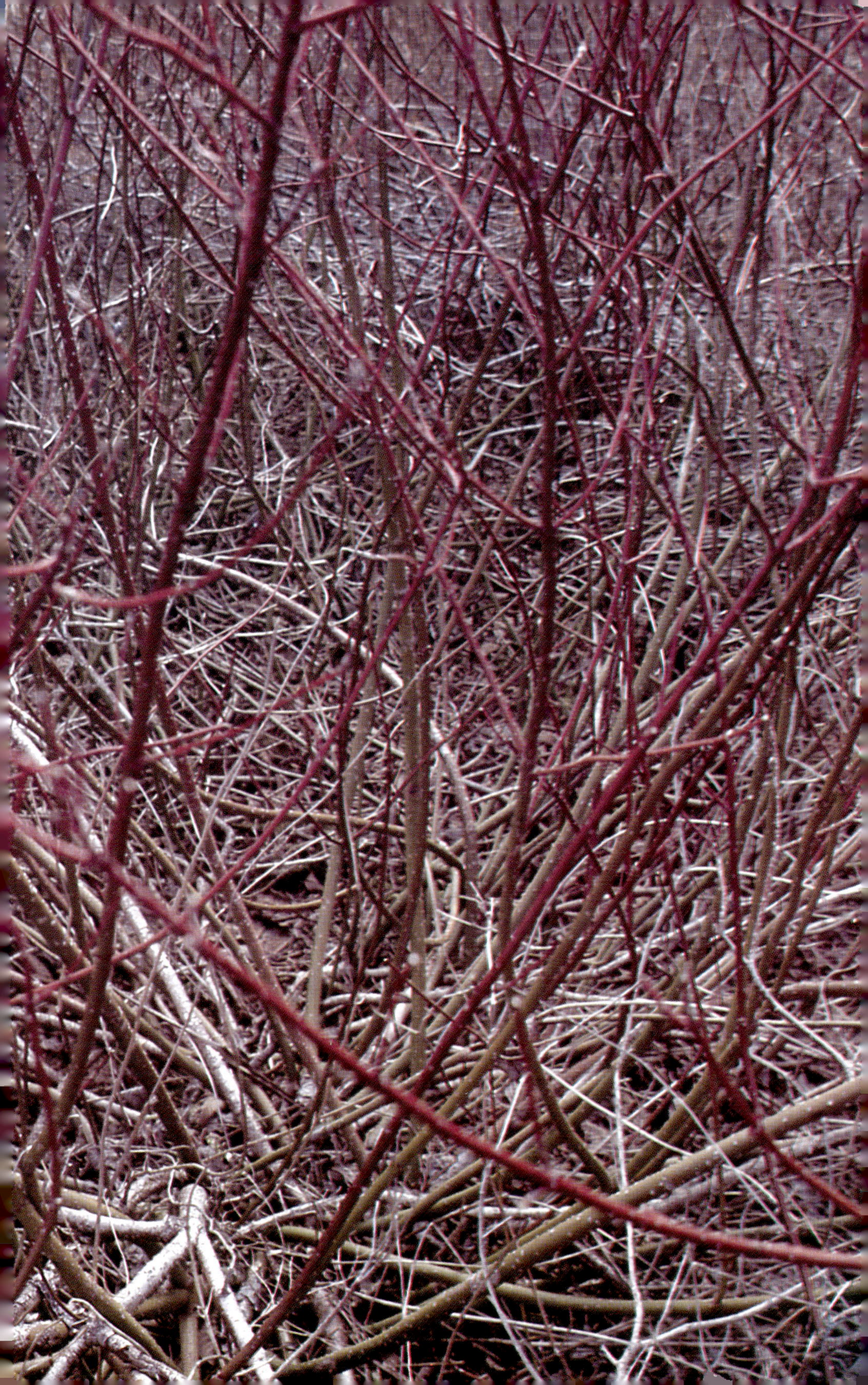

red osier dogwood . . .

It is reported that in Europe the dogwoods were once used to cleanse mangy dogs. Hence the English name. Others suggest the name is a corruption of the word "daggerwood", because its very hard wood was once used to make daggers.

Wherever the name came from, it is clear that the many members of the dogwood family have been around for a long time. Their distribution is worldwide. Of the five species of dogwood shrubs found in New Brunswick, red osier is the most common. Throughout the province it can be found on wet sites, a result of its ability to tolerate flooding.

Red osier will thrive on just about any kind of soil — sand, clay, gravel, loam — acid or alkaline, but it must have adequate moisture. Roadside ditches, wet spots in old fields, and banks of brooks are the natural habitat of the red osier dogwood.

Red osier is highly recommended for planting along stream banks and on the edges of farm ponds. The spreading roots help bind soils to control erosion, while the thick foliage provides summer shade to help maintain cool water temperatures needed for the survival of trout.

Clusters of creamy white flowers appear in June.

as an ornamental . . .

Red osier dogwood's adaptability to almost all soil conditions makes it a natural for landscaping. Rather plain and unspectacular in summer bloom, its main aesthetic appeal is in winter. While most other shrubs are grey and stark, the wine-red branches of the red osier vividly contrast with a background of snow.

Left to nature, red osier dogwood reproduces itself by layering, suckering and by seed dispersed by birds and small mammals. It can also spread by runners, or "stolons", much like strawberry plants.

To plant around the home the best bet is the use of cuttings. In mid-April clip branch tips 10 to 30 cm long. Each clipping or cutting must include three pairs of buds. Plant in the ground with the first two pairs of buds buried and the terminal buds above ground. Survival rate should be fifty to eighty per cent. Two or three cuttings may be planted in each spot to ensure survival of at least one. If they all survive, the weaker plants may be thinned out later. For hedges and stream banks, half-metre spacing is recommended.

wildlife . . .

The small berries are eaten by evening grosbeaks and some ninety other species of songbirds, particularly during the fall migration period. The branches and foliage provide important dense summer cover for hiding and nesting. The flowers are an important source of pollen for honeybees.

Squirrels, chipmunks, raccoons and ruffed grouse all include red osier dogwood fruit in their diet. Moose, deer and snowshoe hares browse the twigs in winter.

Leaves turn red in autumn.

White berries are edible but mealy.

as a medicinal . . .

Ojibwe Indians drank a tea brewed from the red osier dogwood stem for the relief of dysentery. Potawatomi medicine men prescribed the root bark for diarrhoea. For dyspepsia or indigestion the Mohawk tribe drank infusions of red osier bark. The Maliseets of the St. John River valley used a solution made from dogwood bark as an eye bath.

The dried inner bark or leaves, called "kinnikinnik", was a favourite among almost all North American tribes for ceremonial smoking, alone or mixed with tobacco. Some historians attribute its popularity to a slightly narcotic effect.

Red winter twigs bear opposite buds.

Red osier often blossoms again in August.

The bark of the red osier dogwood has been used as a substitute for "cinchona" or quinine to combat fever. Quinine today is a key ingredient in bottled tonic water.

The use of red osier dogwood as a natural red dye is quaintly recorded by Hudson Bay trader James Isham, in 1743:

" . . . . makes an Excellent Dye upon bone, Ivory, Qhils, or cloth & c.: taking the out side bark of, and boiling the under bark, for a Considerable time, over a moderate fire, and Boyl a Comb for half an hour, will come out a fine Deep Red, the root of which tree makes a finer & Deeper Dye than the Bark."

green osier
pagoda tree

*cornouiller à
feuilles alternes*

ALTERNATE LEAF DOGWOOD
(Cornus alternifolia)

Leaf:
Toothless leaves are dark green above, whitish underneath, and alternate. At the ends of branches leaves are so crowded together they may appear opposite. Leaf veins are prominent and typical of all dogwoods, curving upward toward the pointed tip. Leaf size is quite variable.

Stem:
The main trunk is usually straight and rarely over ten centimetres in diameter. The bark on young shrubs is bright green with white streaks. Branches form horizontal tiers, similar to those of open-grown beech, which give the shrub a layered appearance. Overall height is generally four to five metres.

Flower:
In the middle of June flat-topped open clusters of small creamy-white flowers appear at the ends of the branches. Each little blossom contains organs of both sexes.

Fruit:
Clusters of dark blue round berries on red stems mature in late August. Each fruit, less than one centimetre in diameter, bears a single stone. Each stone contains two seeds, one of which usually aborts.

Twig:
Branchlets are greenish-red and shiny, with small alternate pointed buds. The pith is white.

*Immature fruit and leaves
with typical dogwood veins.*

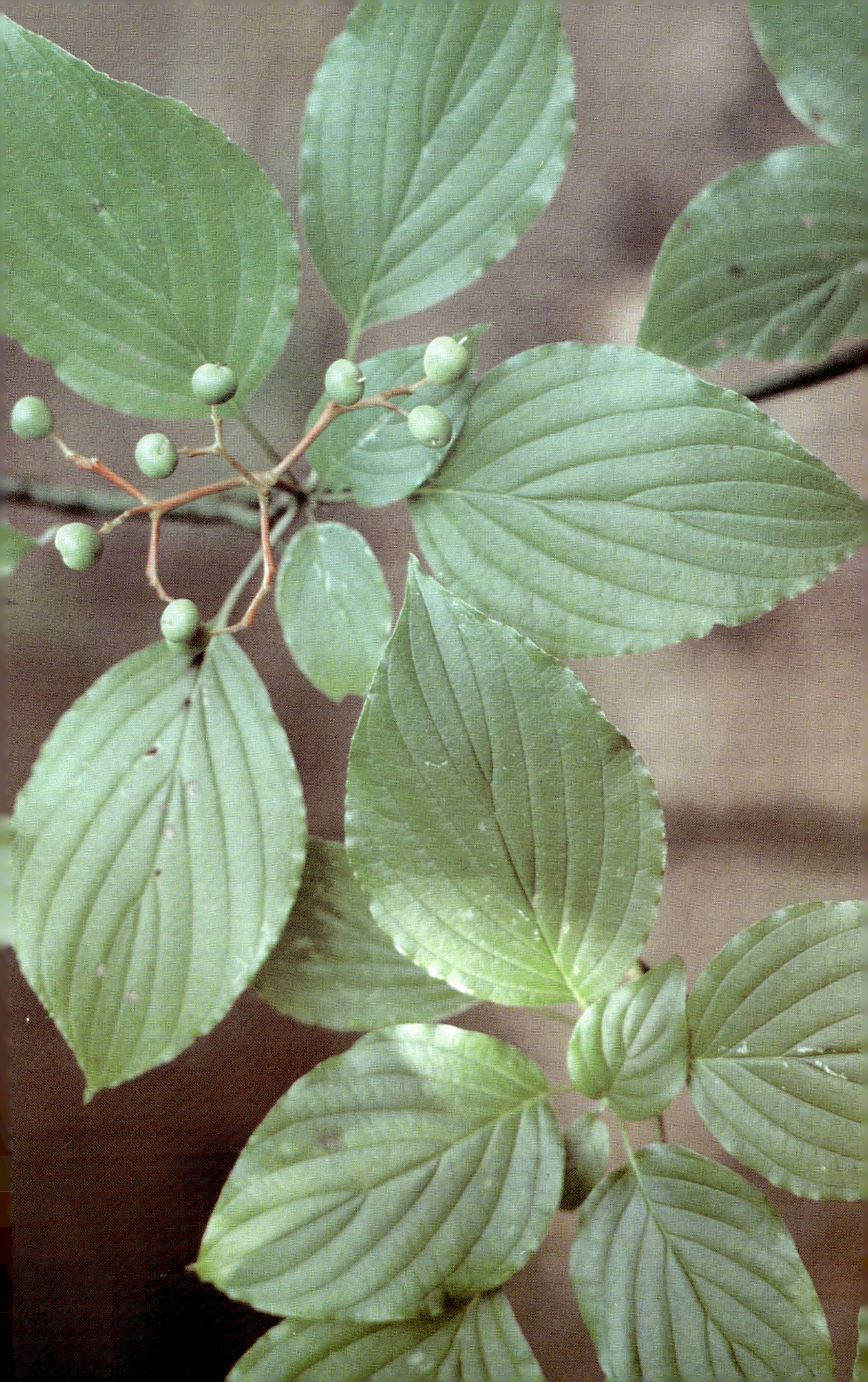

alternate leaf dogwood

Cornus alternifolia is the only member of the dogwood family in America that does not have opposite leaves. However, the clustering of leaves near the ends of the branches does often convey the impression of opposite formation.

The leaves are typically dogwood. Like the red osier dogwood and the diminutive bunchberry, the leaves of this species are toothless, oval and pointed, with the vein pattern characteristic of all dogwoods.

Alternate leaf dogwood can be found throughout the province, yet is rarely abundant in any one area. Very tolerant of shade, it is most at home beneath larger trees in hardwood and mixedwood stands. Shores of streams, open woods and forest borders are its most common habitat, but it will prosper on any fertile, moist, well-drained site.

as an ornamental . . .

The tiered branching effect and handsome foliage make this little tree an interesting ornamental. It may be grown from seed, by layering, or from root cuttings. It can be readily transplanted from the woods when less than one metre high. This should be done in spring, before the buds begin to swell. For optimum growth a nitrogen-rich fertilizer such as urea (34-0-0) or well-composted animal manure is recommended. This species needs plenty of phosphorus, one of the elements necessary for good root development. A fertilizer such as triple superphosphate (0-46-0) or bone meal would lessen the shock of transplanting and stimulate new root growth.

Bark on young shrubs is bright green with white streaks.

Like most species, alternate leaf dogwood is subject to a number of potential insect and disease problems. Twig blight, dogwood borers and other pests may slow down growth and reduce vigor, but these hardy shrubs will generally bounce back once the attack has subsided.

Around the home alternate leaf dogwood will attract over a dozen species of songbirds including warbling vireos. Since leaf-eating caterpillars are staples in the diet of the vireo, it is well worth encouraging these birds to settle around the homestead.

The blue fruit of the alternate leaf dogwood is eaten by ruffed grouse, white-tailed deer and black bear.

of bearings and bear bladders . . .

The small size of the alternate leaf dogwood relegates it to the category of a "non-commercial" tree species. However, in the past its very hard wood was used in the manufacture of friction-reducing components such as bearings. It is reported that the spears of Roman soldiers were fabricated from dogwood.

As a result of spending long hours close to their wood fires, the Indians of the Maritime provinces were regularly afflicted with sore eyes. They found relief by bathing their eyes in a solution made from the bark and roots of alternate leaf dogwood.

A popular pastime of almost all North American Indians was smoking. The bark of the dogwood was scraped, dried and mixed with tobacco to form a pipe blend they called kinnikinnik.

But the most curious of all uses of this shrub was that employed by the Menominee tribe of the U.S. midwest, as described by ethnobotanist Huron Smith:

"The bark of this shrub is gathered to yield a liquid pile remedy. The tepid liquid is placed in a special rectal syringe. This is made from the bladder of the deer or bear, into the neck of which is bound a two inch hollow duck bone. This is tied on with sinew. By compressing the bladder, the liquid is forced into the rectum where it is retained for intervals of half an hour for each application. The bark is also pulverized and put upon a bandage, where a wet application is bound to the anus".

Leaves are commonly crowded together at ends of branches.

hazel
filbert

noisetier à long bec
coudrier
petite noisette

Micmac: malipgantjmosi
Maliseet: mu-li-bekan-sim-os

BEAKED HAZELNUT
(Corylus cornuta)

Leaf:
Alternate leaves are bright green above and paler beneath, pointed at the tip, heart-shaped at the base, and irregularly toothed. Somewhat coarse to the touch and variable in shape, they generally resemble leaves of alder and yellow birch. All three are members of the birch family.

Stem:
The bark on the small (2-3 cm) flexible stems is pale brown and smooth. The shrubs are commonly found in clumps, a result of hazelnut's habit of sprouting from roots or underground stems. Average height is three metres.

Flower:
Male flowers appear in the form of small (2-3 cm long) beige catkins in the fall. Before the leaves open in the spring the catkins release pollen which fertilizes the very tiny red female flowers, located at the tips of the twigs.

Fruit:
The tiny flowers evolve into large round nuts, covered with bright green bottle-shaped bristly husks. The nuts, which ripen in August, may develop singly but more often two or three develop together.

Twig:
The winter twig is slender, yellowish-brown, and often slightly hairy. The buds are round.

Male catkins develop in autumn.

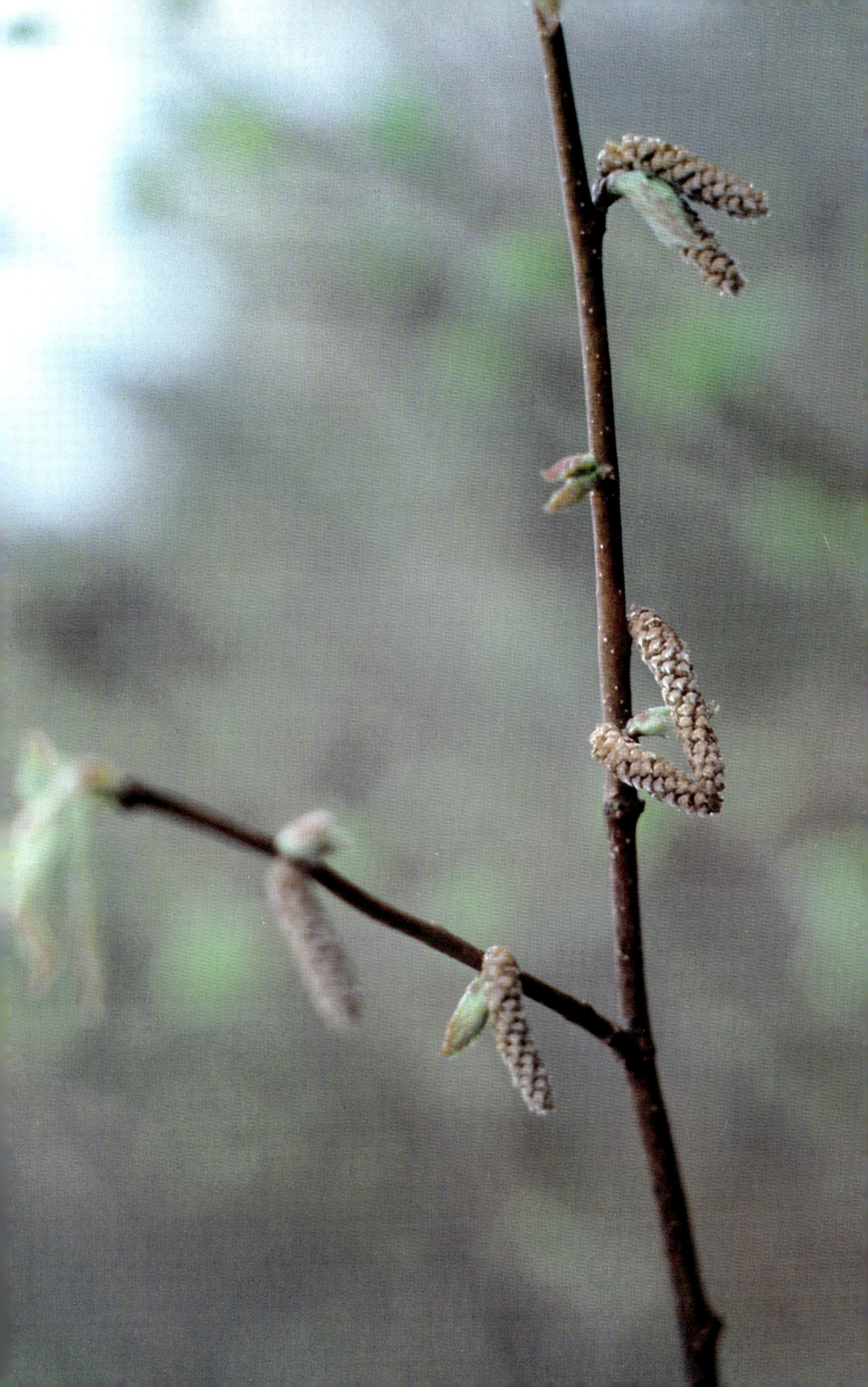

beaked hazel in a nutshell...

Beaked hazel is the only shrub native to New Brunswick which bears an edible nut as its fruit. The hazelnut is smaller in size but just as tasty as the commercially-grown Barcelona filbert, which is found in our supermarkets. Children on the North Shore gather wild hazelnuts in late summer to sell along the roadside.

Beaked hazelnut is considered an early successional shrub, one which is found at the beginning of a forest cycle. It occupies the understorey of the new forest and can survive indefinitely in the shade of taller trees. It plays an important role in the nutrient cycling process. Its leaves are rich in calcium and manganese, and as they decompose they fertilize the trees above them.

It is said that the hazelnut does not like "wet feet", that is, its roots cannot tolerate saturated soil. It thrives on dry, well-drained sites. Roots and underground stems spread prolifically, creating a thick mat just below the surface. A single hazelnut can produce one deep taproot and over thirty metres of shallow roots, all within an area the size of a small room. This extensive network of roots and underground stems can choke out young tree seedlings, and has created a reforestation problem in some areas.

In Canada, the beaked hazelnut is commonly found along roadsides from Newfoundland to British Columbia.

as an ornamental...

Field planting beaked hazel

Hazelnuts are covered with bristly husks.

from seed (nuts) is often unsuccessful, as the germination rate is quite low, and the nuts are favoured fare for rodents. Gather the nuts when the husks develop a brownish tinge at the edges, sun

Leaves resemble those of yellow birch and alder.

dry for a few days and remove the husks. Pack in moist sand and store in the refrigerator. Sow about three centimetres deep in the soil, either in November before the ground freezes or in early spring after it thaws. Hazelnut can also be propagated by grafting, layering or from cuttings.

Once established, beaked hazel requires little care, and should produce nuts within four or five years. It tolerates fairly heavy shade, but can suffer severe winter damage if exposed to winds.

Commercial nurseries usually have several hybrids available which are hardy for cold climates. These are often crosses between the Barcelona filbert of Europe and native hazelnut species.

wildlife and hazelnut . . .

The fruit of the shrub, the hazelnut, is rich in protein and low in carbohydrates, and is a favourite of chipmunks and red squirrels. Once the nuts mature in August, the small rodents eagerly gather them up and store them away for winter.

The buds in winter and the catkins in spring are a valuable source of protein for ruffed grouse, moose, snowshoe hare and American woodcock. Beaked hazel is an important year-round food of the white-tailed deer. Deer eat just about all the plant — leaves, nuts, twigs, catkins, buds, and have been known to browse the stems down to the snowline in winter.

hazelnut and us . . .

In ancient German mythology the hazel was considered sacred. It represented the gods of thunder and the skies, and was believed to provide protection from lightning, snakes, fire and wind. The limbs were used as water diviners, wishing sticks and treasure finders.

On a more mundane level, several Algonquian tribes used hazel twigs bound together to make brooms, and the stems were used for drumsticks. The nuts were eaten by native peoples from coast to coast. Medicinally, the twigs were used for rheumatism, the oil from the nuts for toothache, and the bark to reduce fevers.

Hazelnuts may be used in any recipe calling for nuts, such as cookies, custards, icings or breads.

moosewood　　　*bois barré*　　　*Micmac: wabog*
　　　　　　　　bois d'orignal　　*Maliseet: u-to-kim-os*
　　　　　　　　bourdaine

STRIPED MAPLE
(Acer pensylvanicum)

Leaf:
The large toothed leaves feature three triangular points (lobes) and are rounded or heart-shaped at the base. Like all maples, the leaves are opposite. They turn pale yellow in the autumn.

Stem:
Vertical stripes on the thin bark run the spectrum of colors — red, green, yellow, orange, white, brown, grey. The wood is pinkish brown in the centre (heartwood), with lighter colored sapwood surrounding it. Trees grown from seed have only one main trunk, which rarely grows over 20 cm in diameter. After cutting, several stems may sprout from the stump.

Flower:
Long drooping clusters of bell-shaped yellow-green flowers appear at the ends of branches in late May, before the leaves are fully grown. Male and female flowers often appear on the same tree.

Fruit:
The familiar winged seed common to all maples hang in bunches until mature. In September the seed is released and carried by the wind, spinning to the ground.

Twig:
Winter twigs are red on one side, beige or green on the other, and hairless. Large red buds appear in pairs on opposite sides of the twig.

This small tree derives its name from the multi-colored streaks on the bark.

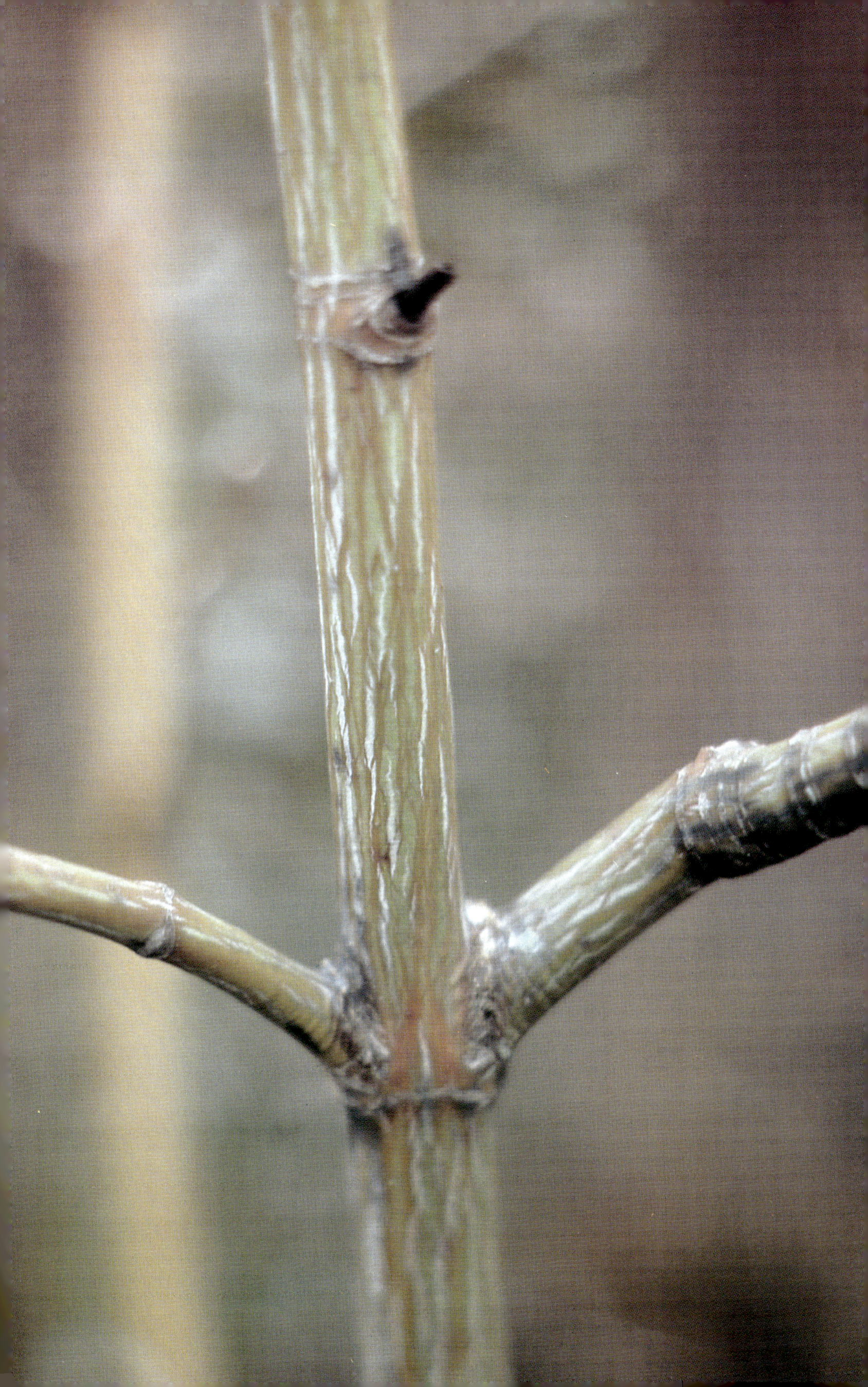

the striped maple story...

One of the smaller members of the maple family, striped maple is almost always found in the shade of larger trees. It prefers moist, well-drained hilly sites, often overshadowed by yellow birch, sugar maple, hemlock or red spruce.

Both striped maple and hobblebush, two very distinct species, are commonly referred to as "moosewood". Both are prime elements in the diet of deer and moose. In fact our word "moose" comes from the Algonquian "mousou", which means "eater of branches". Moose must consume about two kilograms of browse per forty kg of body weight each day to stay healthy during the winter. One technique employed in the management of wildlife is to cut all striped maple whose branches have grown above the point where moose and deer can reach. Like most hardwoods, striped maple will sprout back up the following year, providing high-protein food at a level the animals can reach.

as an ornamental...

Striped maple, with its large leaves and peculiar striped bark, makes an interesting ornamental. Maliseet Indians, however, believed the striped maple was an unlucky tree to have near one's home, claiming the leaves were possessed of a bad spirit, and should never be touched. The Micmacs called it the "starving tree". Superstition has it that he who cuts the striped maple for

Hanging clusters of yellow-green flowers appear in May.

Three-lobed leaves are the largest of the maples.

firewood will starve to death. Even today many Micmacs will not cut a striped maple.

as a medicinal . . .

Among North American Indians the use of emetics was popular to restore health. These were usually concoctions that were so vile or disagreeable they would cause one to vomit, thereby relieving the sufferer of whatever it was that caused him to be ill. Striped maple was one such emetic of the Ojibwa, as evidenced in this Bureau of Ethnology report of 1885:

"The inner bark scraped from four sticks or branches, each two feet long, is put into a cloth and boiled, the liquid which can subsequently be pressed out of the bag is swallowed, to act as an emetic."

Other curative uses of the striped maple included topical application of the leaves for inflamed breasts, poultices of the steeped bark for swelling of the limbs, and bark teas for coughs and colds.

Opposite buds expanding in spring.

45

dwarf maple
virginia maple

érable à épis
plaine bâtarde

MOUNTAIN MAPLE
(Acer spicatum)

Leaf:
Opposite leaves are typically maple-shaped with coarse teeth along the edges and a heart-shaped base. Borne on rather long reddish stalks, the thin leaves are permeated with a network of wrinkled veins. In autumn colours change to yellow or reddish brown.

Stem:
Mountain maple ranges from a straggling shrub to a small bushy tree up to six metres high. Bark on the short trunk is thin, reddish or greyish brown, and usually smooth.

Flower:
Erect clusters of yellowish-green flowers bloom at the ends of branches in late June after leaves have fully grown. Male and female flowers are usually found in the same cluster.

Fruit:
Pairs of bright red winged fruit (samaras) hang in bunches until September. Turning brown at maturity, they are released and spread by the wind.

Twig:
Bright red winter buds develop on slender two-toned twigs — red on the upper side and pale green on the shaded lower side. A coat of fine grey down gives the twigs a slight velvety appearance, particularly near the tips.

Opposite leaves have wrinkled texture.

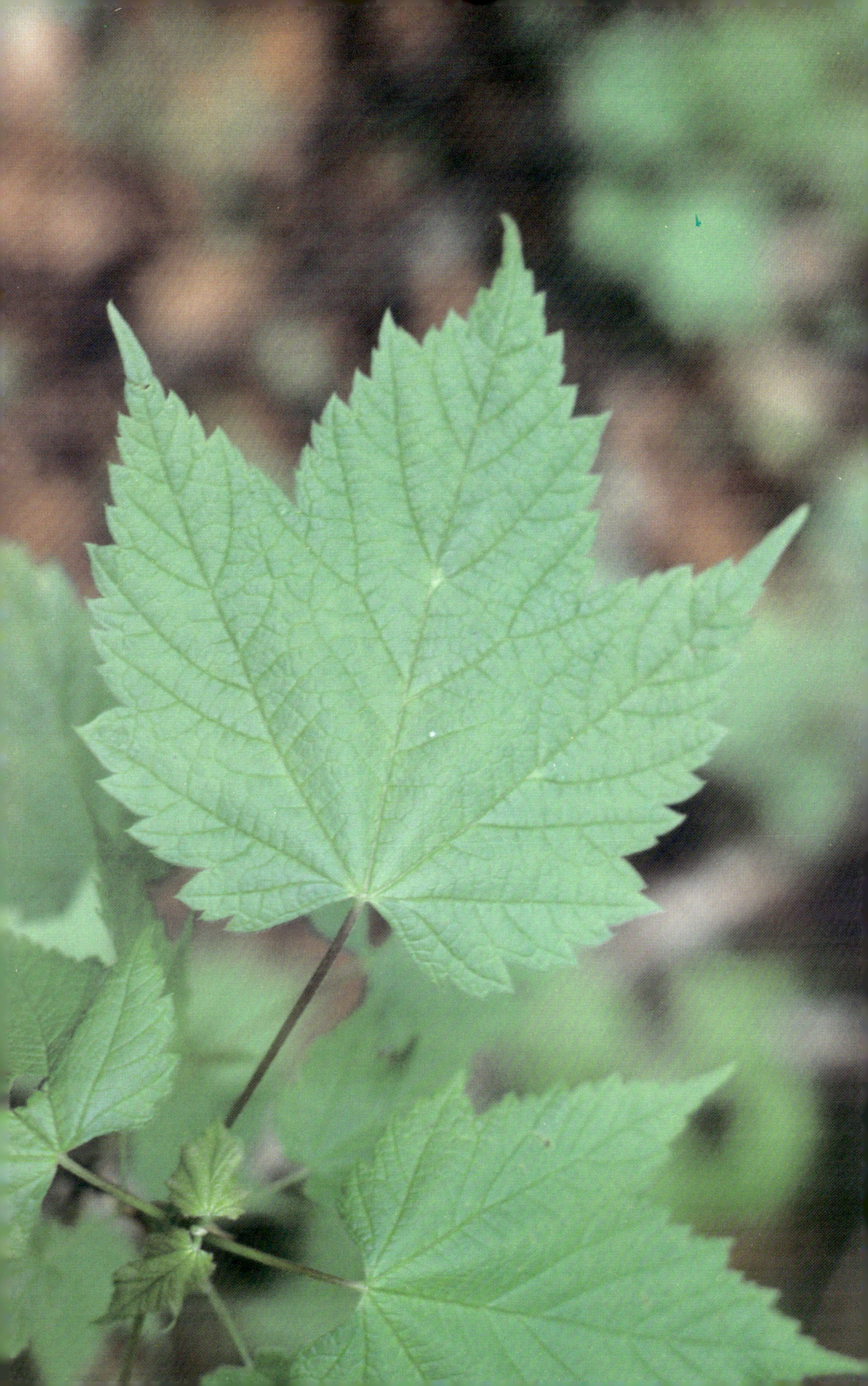

more on mountain maple...

The smallest of our native maples, the mountain maple ranges from Newfoundland to Saskatchewan, and as far north as James Bay. Here in New Brunswick it is found on shaded sites and in damp mixed woods, along stream banks, and on rocky slopes. It is often associated with striped maple and ground hemlock.

On the Green River watershed in the province's northwest, mountain maple has become a major weed problem for foresters. Large tracts of forest harvested in the 1950s and 1960s are now overgrown with the hardy little shrub, which crowds out and suppresses young softwood seedlings. Cutting of mountain maple seems only to encourage vigourous new growth. Controlled burning of cutover sites appears to be the most effective method of controlling this "weed".

wildlife...

Mountain maple can withstand repeated browsing by deer. Up to eighty percent of the tender twigs may be gnawed off over winter, with no apparent deterioration of health and vigour of the shrub. Where present, mountain maple provides deer with one of its most important sources of crude fibre and protein over winter. It is also an important source of nutrition for moose and ruffed grouse.

Although mountain maple is a prolific seed bearer, only a very small percentage of seeds ever germinate. The most common form of reproduction is by stem sprouts just below ground level, or from stumps after cutting. The rapid growth of sprouts can turn a few shrubs into a thicket in a matter of a few years. This species can also reproduce by layering.

Opposite red twigs are covered with fine grey down.

Winged fruit or "samaras" of mountain maple.

as an ornamental . . .

A shady spot should be chosen where the soil is neutral to slightly acid, with plenty of moisture. The shrub will spread and adequate space should be provided.

as a medicinal . . .

Anthropologist H. W. Mechling, who studied the lifestyle of New Brunswick's Maliseet Indians in the 19th century, recorded the following prescription:

"For sore eyes, strip the outside bark from boughs of mountain maple, scrape the inside off and steep a handful in a gill of water. Tie it up in a rag and squeeze the water into the eyes. If the eyes are very sore a poultice is made of it and applied to them".

The bark of the mountain maple was a popular item with the medicine men of many tribes. It was prescribed to relieve liver disorders, to stimulate the appetite, and to treat intestinal worms. South of the border, the bark was gathered and sold to pharmaceutical companies as a substitute for cramp bark (high bush cranberry). It was reported that the bark had a sedative effect on the uterus and was prescribed to prevent miscarriage.

canadian elder   sureau du Canada   Micmac: pogolosganmosi
common elder   sureau blanc   Maliseet: sas-kib-im-os
sweet elder   sirop blanc

ELDERBERRY
(Sambucus canadensis)

Leaf:
Compound opposite leaves contain from five to fifteen leaflets, but usually seven. Leaflets are oval-shaped, toothed and pointed at the tip. They exude a rank odour when crushed. Occasionally the lower set of leaflets may be lobed.

Stem:
Small (up to five cm) stems grow in clumps to an average height of two metres. The brown bark is warty. Young stems have very litle wood, being basically cylinders with a soft white pith.

Flower:
In mid-July parasol-like clusters of creamy white fragrant flowers appear at the tips of the branches. Each tiny (six mm) flower is star-shaped and contains five petals.

Fruit:
In late August and September, heavy bunches of deep purple, almost black berries ripen at the ends of the twigs. Each tiny berry is round, pulpy, juicy and contains three to five seeds.

Twig:
Warty grey-brown twigs bear small opposite buds. There is no terminal bud. The pith is large, soft and white.

Below is a quick key to distinguish between the two species of elder *(Sambucus)* native to New Brunswick.

Elderberry *(Sambucus canadensis)* — flat-topped flower clusters in July, fruit purplish and edible, twig pith white, buds small.

Red-berried Elder *(Sambucus pubens)* — cone-shaped flower clusters in May, bright red fruit (reportedly **poisonous**) twig pith brown, buds very large.

Elderberry clump in flower in July.

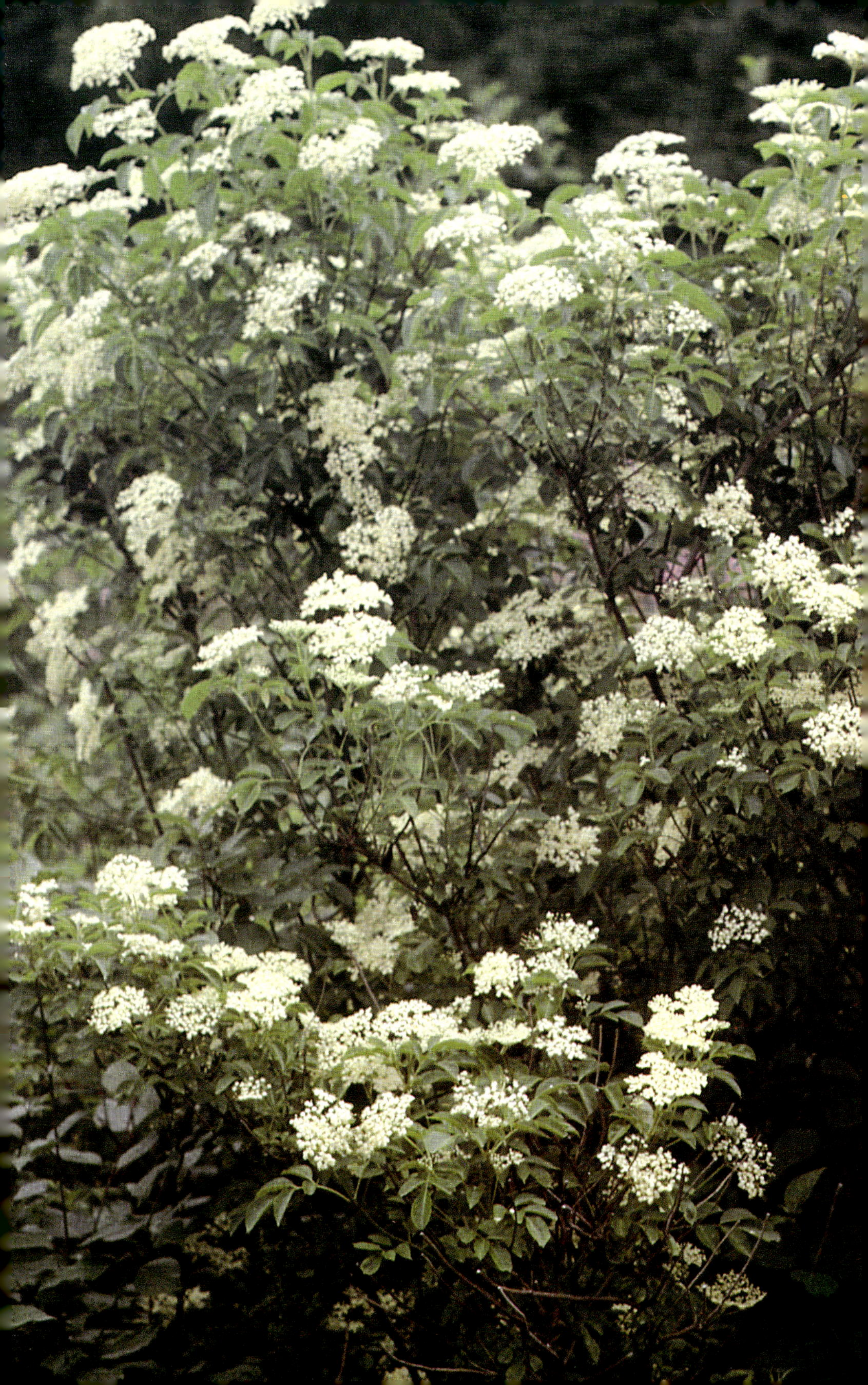

elderberry . . .

Elderberries were first cultivated back in 1761. But they have never achieved the popularity or the commercial success that other wild fruit such as blueberries have. In the early 1960s researchers in Kentville, Nova Scotia developed four cultivars or hybrids of elderberry suitable for commercial production. The new plants bore larger and more plentiful fruit. Bushes laden with eight kilograms of the purple berries were common, and yields of seven tonnes per hectare (three tons per acre) were achieved. But the elderberry, despite its high yield and pleasant taste, still has not caught on with either farmers or consumers.

In the wild, elderberry thrives on moist, fertile soil, and is most frequently found on the banks of roadside ditches and along shores of streams. The shrub spreads by stolons or underground stems, and will sucker several metres from the parent plant, eventually forming a colony or thicket. It may survive in the shade but prefers full sunlight.

as an ornamental . . .

The elderberry is one of nature's gifts from the wild. With very little care and attention the shrub provides a wealth of white blossoms in mid-summer, luxuriant deep green foliage, and clusters of hanging purple fruit in early fall.

Compound leaves usually bear seven leaflets.

To plant elderberry, simply clip branch tips with three sets of buds in early spring. Plant the cuttings directly in their permanent location, preferably after tilling the soil. Bury two sets of buds, leaving the top set exposed.

An alternate method of propagation is to dig up young suckers from around larger shrubs. With a sharp spade cut the underground stems by which they are attached to the parent plant, leaving as much soil as possible on the roots of the little plants, and transplant to their new home. Fertilize with 10-10-10 in a ring around the drip line of the shrub. Apply about 200 grams per year of plant's growth. (e.g. 600 grams the third year).

wildlife...

The quantity of the fruit and its consistency from year to year make the elderberry a favourite with robins and catbirds. Other fruit-eating songbirds like eastern kingbirds, nuthatches, swainson's thrushes and eastern phoebes also relish the juicy black berries. The shrub is often stripped bare within a few days of the fruit ripening. The fruit is also an important September food of ruffed grouse.

Alder flycatchers, goldfinches and yellow warblers have been known to build their nests under the cover afforded by the dense foliage of the elderberry. In winter the twigs are nibbled by moose, deer and snowshoe hares.

Clusters of white flowers are parasol-shaped.

Ends of twigs die back in autumn.

as a medicinal . . .

The early remedies of the Indians were often a curious synthesis of science and superstition. The prescribing of elderberry bark by Maritime Indians is one such case. It was claimed that if the bark were scraped off upward it would act as an emetic, and if scraped downward it would serve as a potent laxative.

Teas made from elderberry flowers were prescribed by both Micmacs and Maliseets to promote sweating, increase the urine flow and induce sleep. Late in the nineteenth century the flowers were listed as an official drug in the U.S. Pharmacopoeia, and in 1868 were included in the official Canadian list of medicinal plants. The fresh flowers or inner bark were blended with lard to produce an ointment for burns, scalds, abrasions and sores.

other uses . . .

Over the years various parts of the elderberry have served a multitude of purposes. Algonquians removed the pith from the twigs and stems and used the hollow cylinders as flutes, whistles and spiles for tapping sugar maples. The soft white pith is the primary source of pith balls used in electrical experiments.

The leaves reportedly have insect-repellent properties and are often mixed with tansy to ward off unwanted insects. Early settlers and Indians alike made a yellow dye from the flowers, a purple dye from the berries and a green dye from the leaves.

the edible elderberry . . .

The raw fruit of the elderberry is somewhat bland but pleasant-tasting and is particularly good when cooked up with more acidic fruits. It is very rich in Vitamin A and Vitamin C and uncommonly high in protein. It contains no pectin.

The virtues of elderberry wine have been extolled in folk and pop songs of recent years. But the gastronomic potential of the fruit does not end there, nor with the conventional elderberry jams, jellies, juices and pies. A review of old cook books reveals such imaginative fare as elderberry pancakes, chutney and even pickled elderberries.

The fruit is not the only edible part of the plant. The unopened flower buds have been used as a substitute for pickled capers. The

flowers may be steeped to brew elder-blow tea. The following inviting recipe was found in *Edible Wild Plants of Eastern North America:*
"the umbels of creamy blossoms make a delicious fritter. Cut at the very height of bloom, soak in brandy with a stick of cinnamon for an hour. Dip each cluster (coarse stems removed) into rich egg batter and drop it in deep hot fat, frying until a light brown. Drain on brown paper, serve sprinkled with powered sugar and orange or lemon juice."

elderberry wine . . .

Pour 4 quarts boiling water over 4 quarts crushed elderberries. Let set for 4 days, strain, and add 4 pounds sugar. Stir well, and let set 4 more days. Add 2 lemons and 2 oranges, sliced. Dissolve 1 package yeast in 4 tablespoons water and pour over 1 slice of toast. Float toast on top of berry juice, and let set 4 more days, or longer, stirring daily. Strain again and bottle. Let set at least 4 weeks before consuming.

courtesy of
Lucy MacPherson, Kingston

When ripe, berries turn dark purple.

red elderberry
stinking elder
poison elder
scarlet elder

sureau rouge
bois de sirop
sureau pubescent

RED-BERRIED ELDER
(Sambucus pubens)

Leaf:
Opposite leaves are compound, containing five or seven leaflets, each 8 to 12 cm long. The oval to lance-shaped leaflets are dark green above, paler and often downy beneath, with sharp teeth.

Stem:
Many small-diameter (up to three cm) stems spread out from the base to a height of three metres. The bark is thin, brown and covered with warts.

Flower:
Oval or pyramid-shaped clusters of creamy-white flowers develop in May. Male and female flowers appear separately on the same shrub. When dry they turn brownish and may remain on the branches for some time.

Fruit:
In mid-July the fertilized female blossoms develop into clusters of small (5 mm) brilliant red berries. Each berry has a yellowish pulp and from three to five seeds. There is some debate as to whether the foul-tasting fruit is **poisonous**.

Twig:
Stout grey-brown warty twigs bear large opposite buds. The buds are greenish yellow and are covered with purple scales. There is no terminal bud. The large reddish-brown pith is soft and spongy and can be easily removed.

One of the first shrubs to flower in spring.

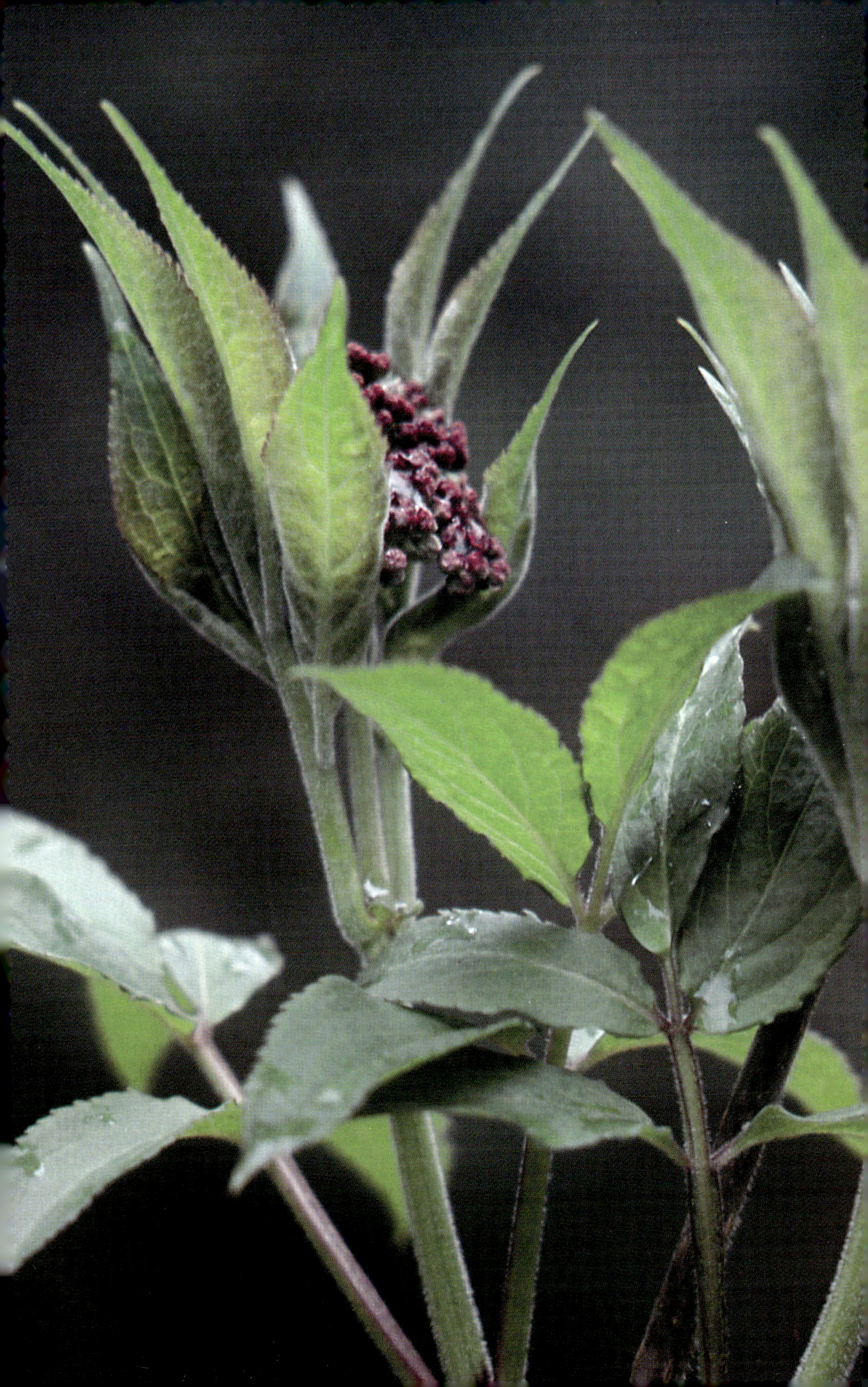

red-berried elder...

The red-berried elder is one of the first plants to stir in early spring. The large globular buds, which have been enclosed in purplish scales all winter, begin to swell in March and by May, develop into clusters of creamy white flowers and large compound leaves.

Red-berried elder thrives on fairly dry sites. It can commonly be found along newly bulldozed woods roads, or in any forest setting where man's activities have unearthed the mineral soil. Once established it grows rapidly for the first few years, eventually spreading by means of underground stems. These stems or rhizomes then send up sprouts several metres away from the original plant. Where conditions are ideal, red-berried elder often form loose colonies.

as an ornamental...

Red-berried elder makes an ideal ornamental, particularly in combination with its cousin the elderberry. In July, when the red-berried elder is bearing its scarlet fruit, the elderberry is just beginning to blossom. Between them, the two shrubs provide handsome foliage, a profusion of white flowers, and bunches of red and purple berries from May until September. They are particularly suited to planting along the edges of ponds.

Red-berried elder may be propagated most simply from cuttings. In early spring, as soon as the frost has left the gound, clip branch tips 40 to 60 cm long, bearing three sets of buds. Plant in a prepared bed or in the garden so that only the top set of buds is above ground. After a year in the bed, the cuttings will have rooted and will be ready for transplanting to their permanent location.

wildlife...

There is a reciprocal relationship between the red-berried elder and the songbird community. Some 23 species of birds consume the fruit. The seed is scattered after it passes through their digestive tracts. The seed germinates, grows quickly, and in a few years the shrub provides both cover and more food for birds.

A number of four-footed

Clusters of bright red berries develop in July.

creatures also eat various parts of the red-berried elder. Squirrels, chipmunks, raccoons, skunks and snowshoe hares eat the berries. In winter, deer and moose will browse the twigs, and ruffed grouse nip off the large buds.

as a medicinal . . .

One of this shrub's nicknames — stinking elder — is deserved. The leaves, flowers and twigs when crushed all have an unpleasant odour. All three are **poisonous** to humans. Menomini Indians of the American midwest brewed a tea from the inner bark, which they used as a last resort in cases of extreme constipation. The liquid acted as a purgative and an emetic, all food within the body being flushed out, often violently. The symptoms described were similar to what we know today as food poisoning.

To determine if the red-berried elder bark was poisonous or not, the Maliseets steeped the bark in water. If it turned green it was poisonous, if it turned milky it was considered safe and was used as an emetic to induce vomiting. Emetics were a common form of medicinal among both the native people and immigrants from Europe.

The soft brown pith of the red-berried elder twig is easily removed, giving rise to the use of the hollow twigs as pipe stems, spiles for tapping sugar maple sap, and toy blow guns for children.

Opposite warty branches are common to both species of sambucus.

fire cherry
bird cherry
wild red cherry
petit merisier
cerisier d'été
cerisier de Pennsylvanie

Micmac: *masgoeesimanagsi*
Maliseet: *muskw-am-os*

PIN CHERRY
(*Prunus pensylvanicum*)

Leaf:
Alternate leaves are long, narrow and pointed at the tip. They tend to hang from the twigs by short stalks. The edges are finely and irregularly toothed. By October, most leaves have turned from bright green to scarlet.

Stem:
Pin cherry has a straight trunk which rises to an open oval-shaped crown. Specimens more than eight metres tall or over 25 cm in diameter are uncommon. The bark is a smooth bronze-red spotted with many oval orange lenticels. The resemblance of the bark to that of young white birch is reflected in the Micmac name "masgoeesimanagsi" which means literally "birch-berry-bush".

Flower:
In May, loose umbrella-shaped clusters of small, five-petalled, white flowers develop on the previous year's twigs. Each tiny flower contains both male and female organs.

Fruit:
By August, each flower cluster evolves into a small hanging bunch of bright red cherries, the stalks of which are attached to the twig at a common point. The juicy cherries (5-6 mm) have an edible but sour pulp and a large round pit.

Twig:
The slender winter twigs are dark red and covered with a thin grey film which can be rubbed off. Alternate buds are small, characteristically with several clustered at the tip. When crushed they exude a bitter almond-like odour.

Clump of pin cherries in winter.

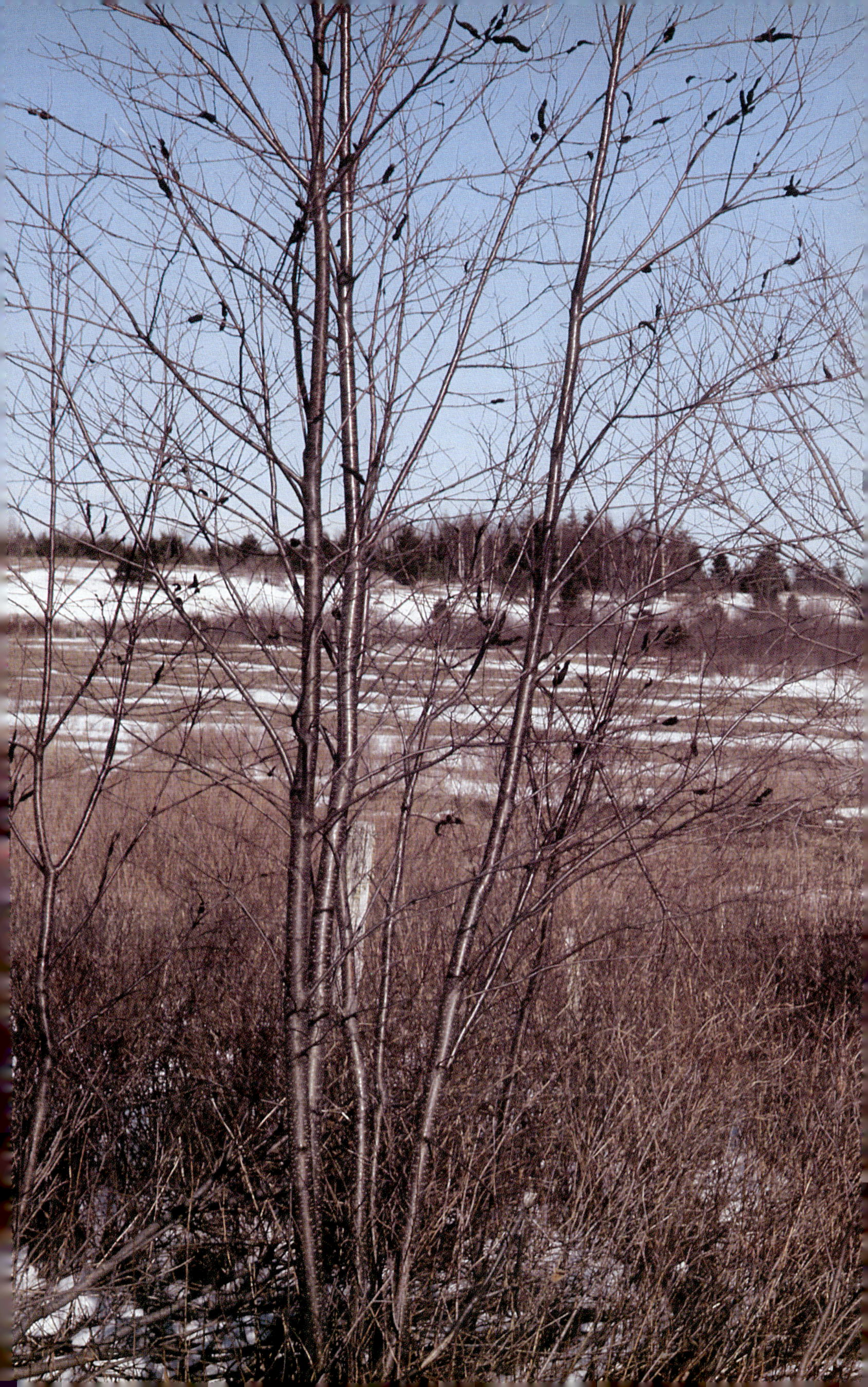

pin cherry . . .

Prunus pensylvanicum certainly deserves the local nickname "fire cherry", for it is one of the most common plants to spring up following a forest fire. Its seed, which may have been lying dormant on the forest floor for years, germinates with the sudden increase in temperature. For the next 20 to 30 years these hardy little trees flourish and serve as a nursery crop for a new generation of longer-lived trees.

The roots of the pin cherry stabilize the soil and prevent erosion, while the annual leaf fall builds up the organic layer of the soil which may have been destroyed by fire. The shade it casts and the shelter it provides are necessary for the germination and initial growth of longer-lived trees. This shade also ensures there will be no future generations of pin cherry, for it cannot survive without full sunlight.

as an ornamental . . .

As a fast-growing, short-lived, undemanding ornamental, pin cherry has few rivals. It is attractive in all four seasons — delicate clusters of white flowers in spring, bright red cherries in August, scarlet foliage in autumn, and wine-red bark and branches throughout the winter months.

There is one drawback. Like its

In autumn leaves turn scarlet.

kin the choke cherry, pin cherry is host to the black knot fungus, which manifests itself in lumpy black growths on the branches. This unsightly fungus weakens the tree and, when plentiful enough, can kill it. It can also spread to nearby cultivated cherry and plum trees. Branches showing the first signs of infection should be cut off about 10 cm before the knot, and the branches burned to prevent reinfection or further spread. This fungus is so common in New Brunswick that the presence of the black growth is one of the quickest means of identifying cherry trees.

Black knot fungus is common throughout the province.

In May, clusters of small white flowers appear.

Tiny red pin cherries are a favourite of wildlife.

pin cherry and wildlife . . .

The ripening of the small red cherries attracts dozens of species of songbirds, including robins and various other thrushes, cedar waxwings, grosbeaks, starlings and catbirds. They consume the flesh and regurgitate or pass the stones, thereby spreading the seed.

The fruit is also eaten by red fox, deer, chipmunks and skunks. Ruffed grouse nibble on the buds in winter, while beaver may eat the bark, especially when poplar is scarce.

Bronze-red bark is dotted with lenticels.

as a medicinal . . .

The fruit of the pin cherry is tart but edible, but the leaves, bark and the pits contain cyanide and are **poisonous.** Native people reportedly derived medicines from these parts, but this is definitely not recommended.

The Maliseets pounded out a powder from the inner bark, which they applied for prickly heat and chafed skin. The inner bark was used as a cough remedy by the Ojibwe, and as an ointment placed on babies' umbilical cords by the Tête de Boule Indians. Teas brewed from the roots were taken for various stomach disorders, both by this province's Indians and by the early Acadian settlers.

Pin cherries are one of autumn's most colourful little trees.

cerisier à grappes Micmac: *eloimanagsi*
cerise sauvage Maliseet: *ulwi-mi-nim-os*
cerisier de virginie

CHOKE CHERRY
(Prunus virginiana)

Leaf:
The dark green egg-shaped leaves are broader towards the tip than they are at the base. The broad end, three to five centimetres across at its widest point, comes to an abrupt pointed tip. Length ranges from five to 10 cm.

Stem:
Choke cherry may have one or more crooked, twisted or leaning stems, the largest of which could measure 10-12 cm in diameter. The smooth, thin, grey bark is inconspicuously dotted with pale orange spots called lenticels. The wood, too small to be of commercial value, is heavy, hard and weak.

Flower:
In late May/early June, when the leaves are half grown, attractive tube-shaped clusters of tiny white flowers appear at the ends of the new shoots. Each little five-petalled flower contains both male and female parts.

Fruit:
Pea-sized red cherries turn purplish at maturity in late August and September. Like the flowers, they are arranged in long nodding clusters on a central stock at the ends of the branches. The fruit has a sharp, sour flavor but is edible. Each choke cherry contains one large round stone or pit.

Twig:
Choke cherry has thicker twigs than any other cherry species. They give off a rank disagreeable odour when crushed. Pale brown pointed buds are arranged alternately on the grey twigs.

Mature cherries are purplish black.

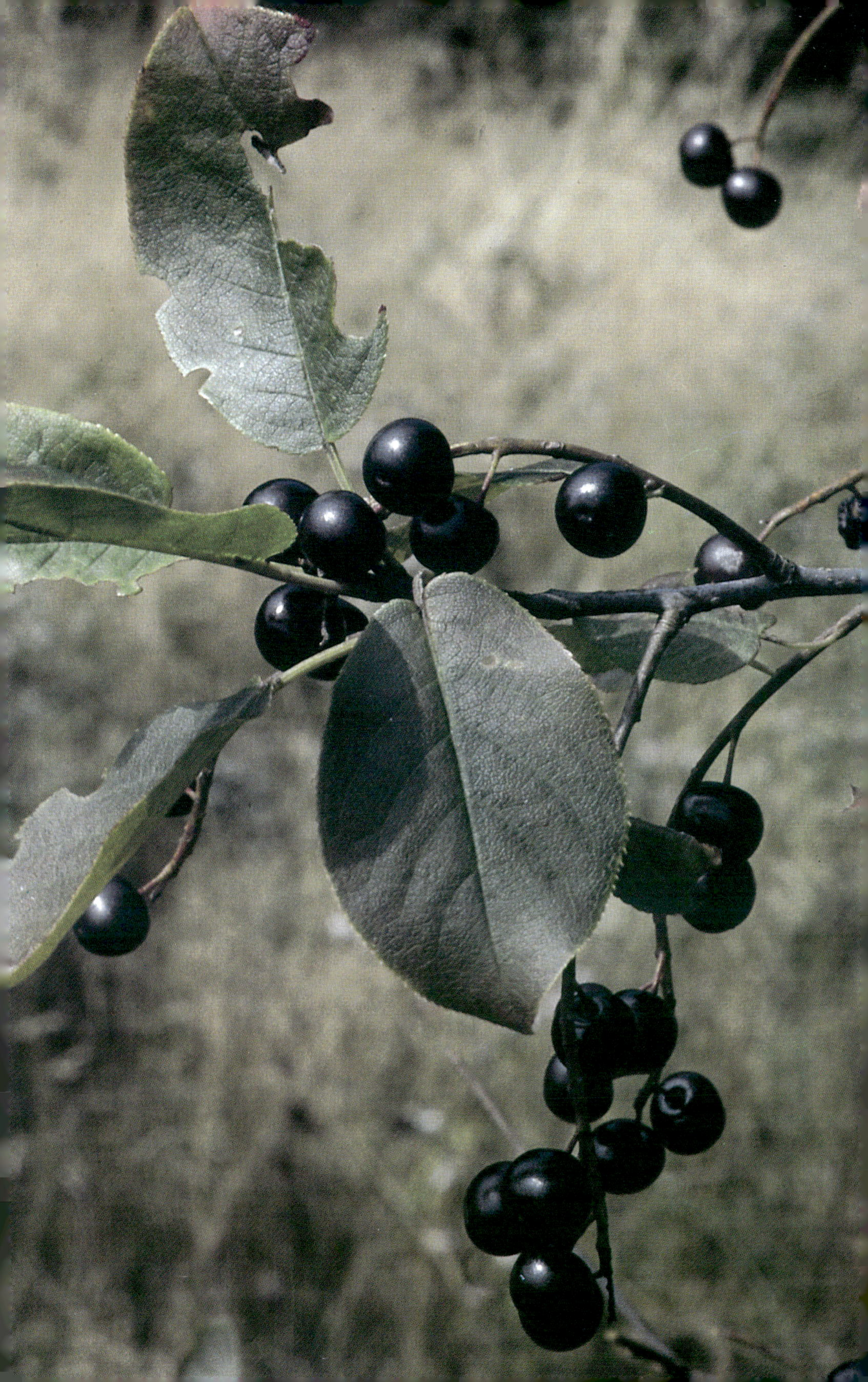

choke cherry . . .

In 1634, American colonist William Wood described how he felt about the taste of choke cherries:

"They so furre the mouth that the tongue will cleave to the roofe, and the throat wax horse with swallowing those red Bullies."

Many a country kid might disagree, but to most palates choke cherries are just a little too sour.

Choke cherry, in one form or another, is the most widely distributed shrub or tree in North America — from Newfoundland to British Columbia, from the Arctic Circle to the deep southern states. In New Brunswick it is one of four species of native cherry, along with pin, black and sand cherry.

Choke cherry prefers moist, well-drained soil and full sunlight, and will grow best under these conditions. But it will grow in almost any environment, even on poor, almost sterile soil, or in the shade of larger trees. It can sometimes be found growing on rock piles created when settlers cleared the land for farming. In fact, wherever birds or other small forest folk drop the seeds, choke cherry is likely to spring up.

Once established, choke cherry is very competitive, crowding out other vegetation. Fast growth of suckers and sprouts from the roots can soon form dense thickets. It is commonly found on old fields, along roadsides and stream banks, and on farm waste areas, especially around barns and in fence rows.

Choke cherry is a hardy shrub. Despite its susceptibility to a number of insect and disease problems, it still manages to persist. It is one of the favourite hosts of the black knot fungus, which manifests itself in lumpy black growths on branches, aptly nicknamed "crotte de chien" in French. It is also the host of the notorious X-disease, which doesn't seem to bother the choke cherry, but can kill nearby peach and commercial cherry trees.

As if that weren't enough, choke cherry is considered a delicacy by eastern tent caterpillars, which pitch tents among its branches and devour every leaf.

Choke cherry twig is stouter than that of other cherries.

as an ornamental . . .

Because of these problems choke cherry is not recommended as an ornamental. But perhaps an even more significant drawback is the toxicity of its leaves. They contain prussic acid, a cyanide compound, which can be **poisonous** to humans and livestock alike. Five to ten grams of choke cherry leaves consumed by a small child could be fatal. There have been many

Clusters of choke cherry flowers are most attractive.

examples of livestock poisoning from choke cherry leaves. The same poison, incidently, is contained in the stones of cherries, peaches, and plums, and in apple seeds.

Choke cherry has been planted to stabilize soils, as windbreaks and to attract wildlife. A good crop of fruit most years provides food for over thirty species of game and songbirds, as well as a number of small mammals. In fall and winter the twigs are eaten by red fox, skunk, chipmunk and partridge.

as a medicinal . . .

The Maliseet name for choke cherry was "ulwiminimos", literally "berry that binds the bowels together". In the fall Maliseets gathered the inner bark and steeped it to make a tea used to treat diarrhoea. This practice they had in common with such widely scattered Algonquian bands as the Cree in Saskatchewan, the Menominee in Wisconsin, and New England's Penobscots. In fact the choke cherry was probably the most utilized medicinal tree or shrub in North America. It has been included in the Pharmacopoeia, the United States official listing of drugs.

Native remedies were quite varied. They used choke cherry as a tea for indigestion, as a tonic during pregnancy, and as a gargle for sore throat.

Choke cherries were dried and mixed with meat and animal fat to make pemmican, the food staple of many tribes in winter.

may-apple *aubépine* Micmac: *gôôgmanagsi*
thorn-apple *senellier* Maliseet: *jikun-i-akw-em-os*
  pommette

HAWTHORN
(Crataegus spp.)

Leaf:
Leaves are relatively small, alternate, irregularly toothed and often lobed. Leaf shape varies, often on the same shrub. They are commonly glossy green above, duller and slightly hairy beneath.

Stem:
The young bark ranges from dark red to grey and is dotted with pale lenticels. On older trees it becomes scaly or shreddy. Height varies but rarely exceeds seven metres. The wood is hard, heavy and tough. The sapwood is pale, the heartwood is reddish.

Flower:
In May and June, showy clusters of white flowers appear at the ends of the branches. Each component flower has five round petals, and is perfect, i.e., contains both male and female parts. Some hawthorn flowers have a slightly unpleasant smell. The famous pilgrim ship "Mayflower" was named after the blossom of the English hawthorn.

Fruit:
Red or orange fruit resembling miniature apples develop in August and September. Each "haw" contains 1-5 large seeds surrounded by a yellowish pulp. Fruit frequently remain on the branches long after leaf fall.

Twig:
Zig-zagging branches are armed with stiff thorns up to 8 cm long. These sharp-pointed spines are smooth, as if polished. Winter buds are small, round and brown.

Fruit of the hawthorn resemble small apples.

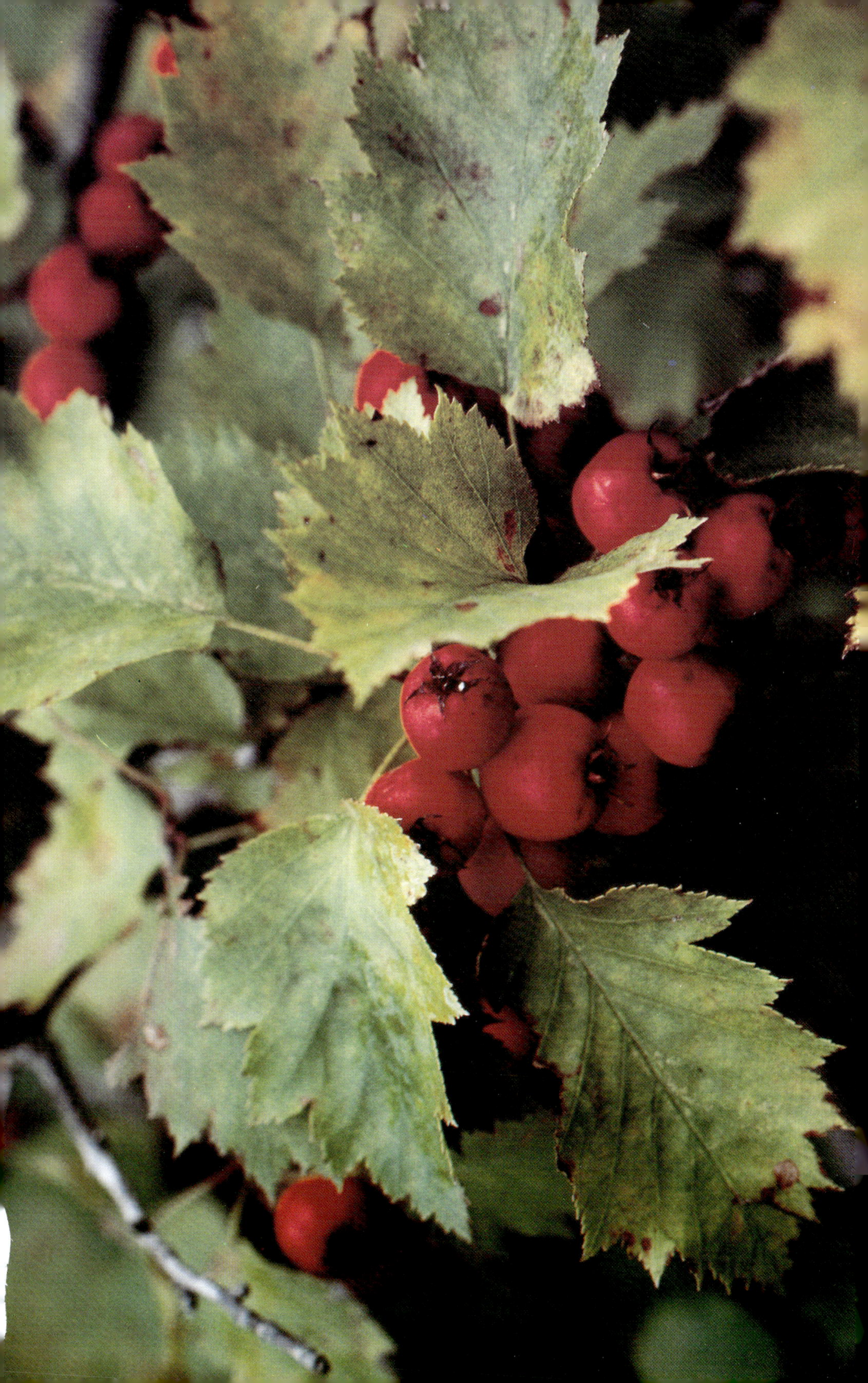

hawthorns by the hundreds . . .

It is not hard to recognize a hawthorn — its long sharp thorns are unique in the shrub world. But determining *which* species of hawthorn is another matter. In North America there are between 200 and 1,200 different kinds of hawthorn. Not only do the experts disagree on distinctions between species, but they do not even agree on how many species there are. For the purpose of this book all hawthorns are treated as one group.

The hawthorns are members of the rose family, which also includes cherries, plums and apples. There is a distinct family resemblance between the haw, (the fruit of the hawthorn) and the apple. In fact a common local French name for the haw fruit is "pommette", literally "small apple".

Hawthorns are most likely to be found on abandoned pastures, on forest edges and on stream banks. On old fields they are found in the early stages of the long process of farm land reverting back to forest. For this reason they are called an "early succession" species and fill the role of a nursery crop. Tree seed blown in from the side germinates under the protection of the hawthorn, only to push up through the shrubs and eventually shade them out. Since hawthorns are intolerant of shade, they lose vigour and ultimately die off, leaving a stand of longer-lived, more tolerant trees.

Hawthorns can adapt to a wide range of soil conditions, but seem to do best on moist to wet sites. They are most commonly found on sites where wild crab-apple, blackberry and the dogwoods also thrive.

Hawthorn leaves are rather irregular in shape.

as an ornamental . . .

Although generally regarded by farmers as a weed at best, and at worst a hazard to themselves and their livestock, native hawthorns do have the potential to be rather attractive ornamentals. The plentiful showy white flowers in the spring, the green summer foliage, and the crimson fruit in autumn make the hawthorn a most worthwhile choice in any landscaping venture.

hawthorn and wildlife . . .

Hawthorn hedges, because of their dense branching, heavy foliage and thorny defences provide excellent sanctuary for nesting birds such as grey catbirds. Game birds like American woodcock and ruffed grouse may hide and rear their young amid the dense cover of hawthorn.

While fruit yields vary from year to year, there is almost always an ample supply for birds such as cedar waxwings, robins and pine grosbeaks. White-tailed deer eat not only the fruit, but also the leaves and twigs.

Unfortunately the leaves are also a favourite of the eastern tent caterpillar, which build their nests in the crotches of the branches and can devour all the leaves on a shrub in a matter of a few days. Pesticide is one way to protect ornamentals. Picking off the egg masses which encircle the twigs, before they hatch in the spring, is a good alternative.

medicinal and other uses . . .

Of 39 species of hawthorns tested, the fruit of 15 proved to have some ability to lower blood pressure. The U.S. Drug Dispensatory at one time listed hawthorn fruit as being astringent and having heart tonic properties.

Native Americans found numerous uses for different parts of the shrub. The leaves and flowers were steeped in boiling water to produce a cough medicine. People of the Meskwaki tribe consumed the unripe fruit to

A profusion of white blossoms in spring.

ease bladder problems. The Chippewas drank a tea brewed from the roots to relieve back pain, while the Micmac steeped the twigs to make a tea for rheumatism.

The flavour of the hawthorn fruit varies with the species, but all haws are edible. The fruits are high in sugar, low in fat and protein, and contain pectin. They make excellent jelly or marmalade. Traditionally Indians would dry the fruit, press it into cakes and store it for winter use.

The thorns of the hawthorn were employed by Indian women as awls to sew leather. The dense and durable wood was often carved into tool handles. The wood of the hawthorn, though

Branches are armed with long thorns.

Haws are eaten by a number of songbirds.

seldom large, makes excellent firewood. At one time it was burned to melt pig iron.

hawthorn purée...

Put 1 litre cleaned haws in saucepan, cover with cold water, and let stand overnight. Without straining, simmer for 15 minutes. Mash then simmer for another 10 minutes. Remove from heat and let stand for 5 minutes. Strain through a sieve, retaining as much purée as possible.

The purée can be used in cakes, biscuits, jams, jellies, etc. For a healthful tea add 1 tablespoon hawthorn purée to 1 cup hot water. Add honey to taste.

courtesy of
Georgina Larocque, Campbellton

ground hemlock *sapin traînard* Micmac: gasteg
american yew *if du canada* Maliseet: to-kun-as-tekw
dwarf yew *buis de sapin*

CANADA YEW
(Taxus canadensis)

Leaf:
Flat evergreen needles are similar in appearance to those of balsam fir and eastern hemlock. They are dark glossy green on top, pale yellow-green beneath, and up to two centimetres in length. Unlike fir and hemlock, the needles taper to a sharp tip.

Stem:
Numerous bow-shaped stems spread horizontally from the base of the shrub, then curve upwards to an average height of one metre. The wood is tough and flexible. Inner bark is red.

Flower:
Separate male and female flowers are small and inconspicuous. Both may appear on the same plant, usually in May.

Fruit:
Waxy red berries appear in mid-summer on sides of twigs. Each cuplike fruit contains one hard seed. The stone reportedly contains the alkaloid "taxine", and is **poisonous**. But the flesh of the berry tastes sweet and honey-like, and is quite edible. Yew is seldom a prolific bearer of fruit.

Twig:
One - and two-year-old twigs are shiny bright green, older twigs become brown and scaly.

Waxy red fruit is cup- shaped.

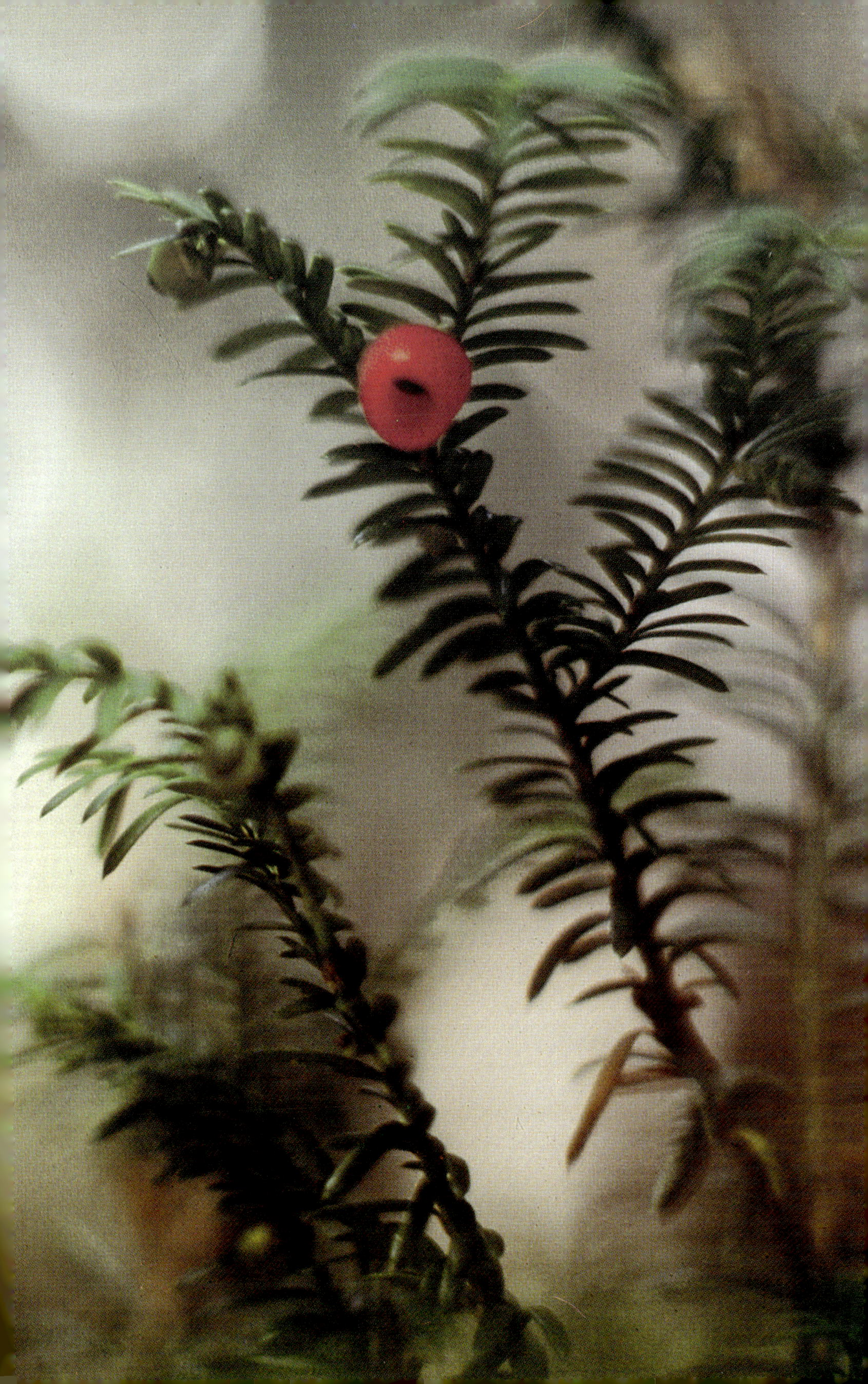

the wonders of yew . . .

The smallest member of the yew family, the ground hemlock is usually found in the shade of larger forest trees. It seldom reaches a height of two metres, and individual stems are normally less than two centimetres in diameter. Its common habit of layering helps it spread throughout the forest floor, providing a loose thicket of year-round greenery. Ground hemlock prefers moist rich soils, but even under such ideal conditions it grows very slowly.

Moose include ground hemlock in their diet but it has few other uses by wildlife species.

Although not common, ground hemlock is used for making Christmas wreaths.

as a medicinal . . .

In the world of natural medicines the root of the ground hemlock was one of seven special herbs which made up the Micmac magic healing potion. It was taken both internally, as a tonic, and externally as a dressing for a variety of conditions.

There were numerous uses of ground hemlock by both Micmacs and Maliseets in the process of childbirth, and to relieve pain of afterbirth. Early Acadian women drank a tonic of ground hemlock to regulate the menstrual cycle. In the southern states, the yew reportedly had some degree of popularity among slaves to induce abortion.

The twigs and needles, when steeped, produce a hot beverage rich in Vitamin C, which was used

Bowed stems are usually less than one metre high.

Erratum

The following text should replace the last three paragraphs on page 79.

By far the most valuable use of ground hemlock today is as a cancer drug. When the National Cancer Institute began investigating native plants in the early 60's, Pacific yew bark proved effective in clinical trials. But concern over overharvesting the uncommon little tree led to research on other yews, including ground hemlock.
Today branch tips are harvested commercially and sustainably, and processed into paclitaxel to treat ovarian and other forms of cancer by chemotherapy.

Needles are similar to those of hemlock.

to treat scurvy as well as the common cold. Note: wilted foliage is **poisonous.** The leaves, mixed with those of cedar and hemlock, were regularly used in native peoples' sweat baths, a practice common to almost all Indian tribes across North America. On the Restigouche in 1691, pioneer priest Chrestien Le Clercq described the forerunner of today's fashionable sauna:

"The sweat house is a wigwam covered with bark, or with skins of beaver and moose, and so arranged that it has no opening whatever. In the middle thereof the Indians place some hot stones which heat those inside so much that water soon starts from all parts of their bodies. They throw water upon those hot stones, whence the steam rises to the top of the wigwam, then it falls upon their backs, much like a hot and burning rain . . . Then rising quickly from this wigwam they throw themselves into the river in order to cool themselves".

The addition of roots, bark and leaves to the water provided a medicated steam bath used for a variety of ailments from rheumatism to fevers.

Jim Crowe, a multiple sclerosis victim living in Sussex, attributes his success in battling the disease to a tonic prescribed to him a long time ago by a Gagetown Maliseet Indian. The recipe is:

Add one oz. each of freshly-cut ground hemlock and cedar to one qt. cold water. Boil, cover and steep 4 to 5 hrs. Strain and bottle. Drink one oz. a day, 6 days a week.

Mr. Crowe claims it will prevent spasms, depressions, migraines and deep internal infection.

shadbush billberry *amélanchier*
juneberry sugar plum poirier   Micmac: *gelmoetjmanagsi*
saskatoon indian pear petite poire
                         bois de flèche

SERVICEBERRY
(Amelanchier spp.)

Leaf:
Serviceberry leaves vary in shape from nearly round to long oval and pointed. A few species are heart-shaped at the base but most are rounded. The alternate leaves may be as small as four cm and as large as 10 cm. Leaf edges are always toothed.

Stem:
The serviceberries range from small shrubs to trees over 10 metres in height. Young bark is light grey and smooth and streaked with darker vertical lines. Older bark becomes scaly. The wood is hard, heavy, tough and close-grained. The heartwood is dark reddish-brown and the sapwood is pale.

Flower:
Serviceberries bloom in May, before the leaves have fully grown. Individual white flowers have five long delicate petals. They most commonly appear at the ends of the branches.

Fruit:
When ripe in July, the edible berries are round, dark purple, and topped with five tiny withered flower parts. Each pea-sized fruit contains from four to 10 seeds. *Amelanchier* berries are sweet and usually juicy, with a pleasant odour.

Twig:
Slender winter twigs are often coated with whitish film. They bear long pointed buds, similar to those of beech, and have a slight almond-like taste. The pith is green and is five-sided.

Leaves turn rust-red in autumn.

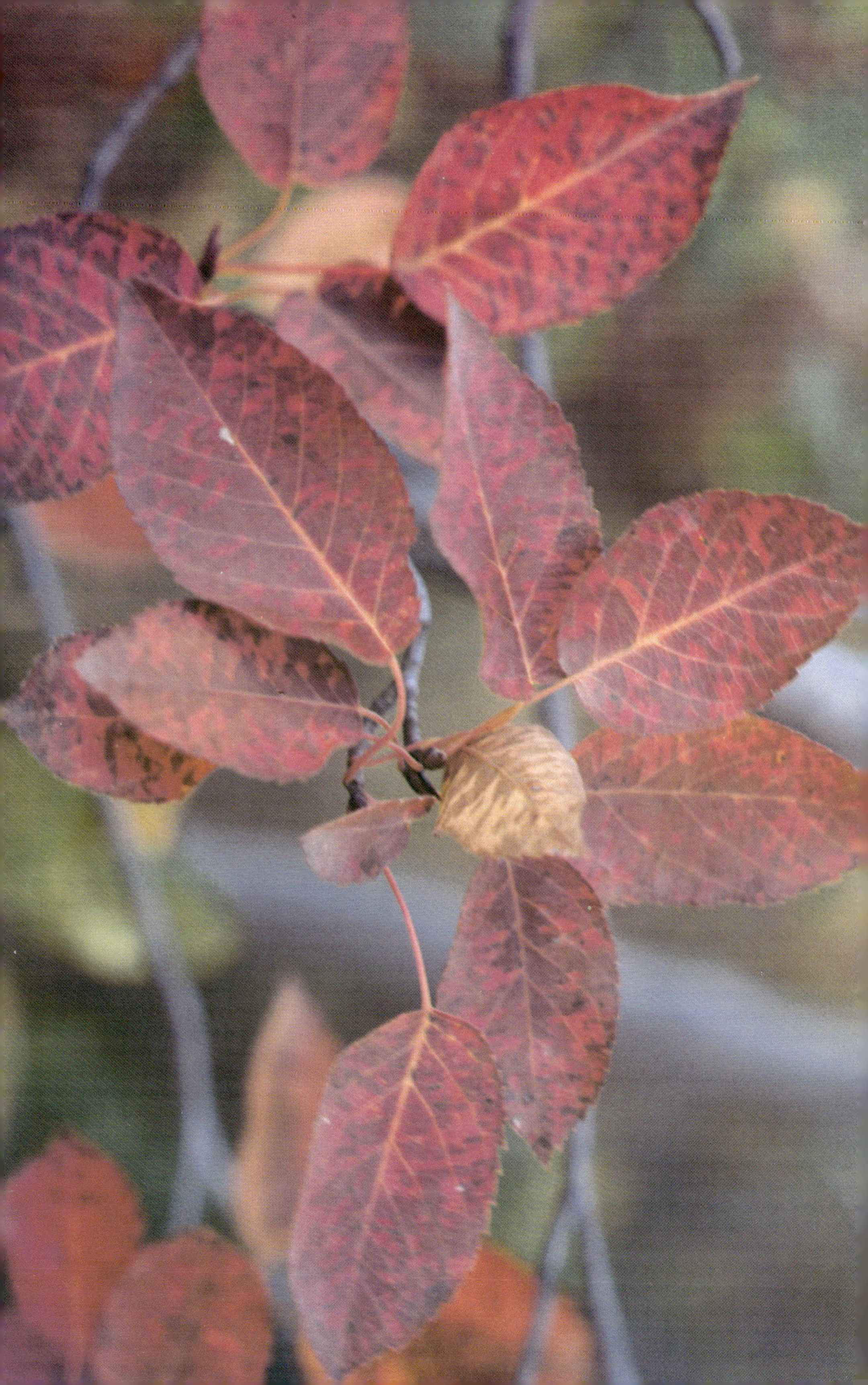

an *amelanchier* by any other name...

The *amelanchiers* present an exercise in frustration to the scientist who must categorize and classify the numerous species. Botanists have never been able to agree on how many species there are, nor can they agree on the characteristics which distinguish one species from another.

One theory has it that certain species of serviceberries have cross-bred or hybridized over a period of several centuries. As the white man cleared forest land for farming, extensive new areas of habitat suitable for serviceberry were opened up. This provided the opportunity for previously isolated species to come together and interbreed. The process was facilitated by insects carrying pollen from one species to fertilize the flowers of another.

Depending on which expert one listens to, there are from eight to 18 species of serviceberry in North America. At least eight of these are native to New Brunswick. To confuse the issue a little more, there are probably a dozen different local names for the genus, many of which do not necessarily correspond to the scientific names.

Furthermore, there is extraordinary variation of foliage not only within the same species, but often on the same plant. This prompted one old forestry professor to suggest, "If you're in the woods and

White flowers develop with new leaves.

you run into a tree you can't identify, it's probably an *amelanchier*."

as an ornamental . . .

Serviceberries come into their own in the spring. Before the leaves have fully unfolded, they put forth an elegant display of white blossoms. In autumn the foliage turns to various shades of amber, rust, red and purple.

The serviceberries are generally hardy ornamentals. Successful plantings in urban centres have indicated the plants' resistance to air pollution. They may be propagated from seed, cuttings, or from suckers.

Grey bark bears dark streaks.

When ripe, fruit turns from rosy red to purple.

Serviceberry leaves are quite variable in shape.

serviceberries and wildlife . . .

A host of songbirds including hermit thrushes, robins, chickadees, catbirds, blue jays and woodpeckers quickly gobble up the juicy berries as soon as they ripen in July. Furbearers large and small, such as bears, squirrels and martens are fond of the fruit as well. In winter the slender twigs and long narrow buds are eaten by moose, deer, red fox, snowshoe hare and eastern flying squirrels.

The early blooming of the serviceberries in spring provides an important source of pollen and nectar for bees and other insects.

as a medicinal . . .

There are few documented uses of the serviceberries for medicinal purposes by the Indians of North

Buds are long and pointed.

Profusion of flowers in spring make serviceberries an attractive ornamental.

America. The fruit, however, was a staple in the diets of many tribes. The berries were eaten raw, cooked and preserved. Serviceberries, or "saskatoons", were blended with strips of meat and animal fat to make pemmican. White explorers followed the example of the natives, calling the fruit "little pears." The name "petite poire" still persists with today's francophones.

other uses . . .

The wood of the serviceberries is hard, heavy and strong. That of the larger species has been used to make tool handles and fishing rods. The Cree Indians used serviceberry wood for arrows, giving rise to the voyageurs naming it "bois de flèche."

snapping hazel *hamamélis de virginie* *Micmac: aoeligtj*
spotted alder *café du diable*
winterbloom

WITCH HAZEL
(Hamamelis virginiana)

Leaf:
The alternate leaves are irregular in shape, with wavy edges and an uneven or asymmetrical base. Leaf veins are straight and rather conspicuous. Leaves are sparse, giving the shrub a straggly appearance.

Stem:
The trunk is short and crooked, with long forked branches. The bark is brown and smooth, the inner bark reddish purple. The wood is hard and heavy, and very close grained. Average height is four metres.

Flower:
Witch hazel is our only shrub or tree which flowers in autumn. About the time of leaf fall, open clusters of bright yellow flowers appear on the twigs. Each stemless blossom has four slender ribbon-like petals two or three cm long.

Fruit:
The flowers develop into nut-like capsules which are covered with greyish down. They remain intact on the branches until maturity the following autumn, when they pop open and shoot out two shiny black seeds. The open pods often persist on the shrub throughout the next winter.

Twig:
The slender twigs are yellowish-brown. The winter buds are stalked, flattish and slightly curved, and are covered with yellowish down.

Each flower bears four yellow ribbon-like petals.

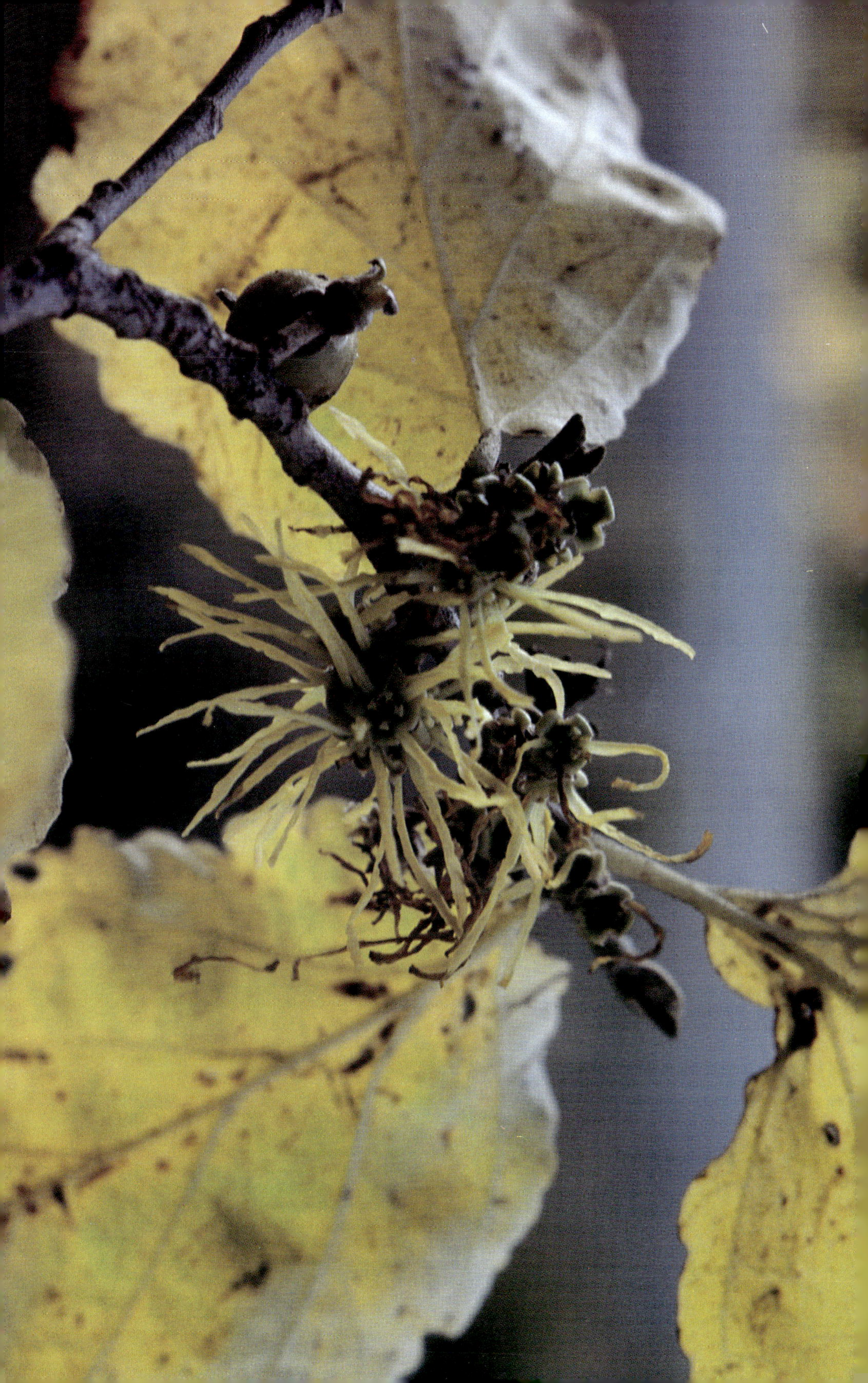

witch hazel . . .

Witch hazel is an uncommon shrub in New Brunswick, this being the most northern limit of its range. It does not grow north of the Miramichi. But it has been included in this collection for two reasons. First, its curious flowering and fruiting habits are truly unique in the plant world. Second, the medicinal properties of witch hazel have spawned a multi-million dollar industry.

Witch hazel is a botanical oddity. It is the last of our native plants to flower. At the time when most deciduous trees and shrubs are shedding their leaves and entering dormancy, witch hazel blossoms profusely. The yellow flowers develop into nut-like capsules which remain on the shrub until the following autumn. At that time they split open, often with an audible snap, and eject two tiny seeds which have developed inside. The capsules remain on the plant, open and empty, often until the following autumn.

This strange little tree requires a damp rich soil and is most often found along the edges of the woods, in forest openings and along roadsides. It frequently thrives in the shaded understorey of hemlock, cedar and yellow birch, accompanied by mountain maple, hobblebush or striped maple.

as an ornamental . . .

Witch hazel is a must for home-owners interested in landscaping with native plants. An interesting but somewhat awkward and straggling shrub most of the year, the witch hazel's reward comes in the fall. As if it were spring in October, clusters of yellow flowers adorn the branches, providing a breath of colour when most other hardwoods are stark and grey.

Transplanting seedlings from the wild is a good method of propagation. In late summer, search in the vicinity of a mature witch hazel for young seedlings. Tag or ribbon them so they will be easily identifiable without their leaves next spring. In April dig up the seedlings, being careful not to break off any roots. The more soil left on the tiny rootlets, the less shock to the plant. Place in a bag, transport to their new home, and replant. Witch hazel is a slow grower, but is quite hardy and will prosper under shady conditions.

Sparse leaves give witch hazel a straggly appearance.

Leaves are rather irregular in shape.

Brown bark is relatively smooth.

as a medicinal . . .

In 1892 Charles Millspaugh, in his classic treatise *American Medicinal Plants* stated: "The many varied uses of a watery infusion of Witch-hazel bark were fully known to the aborigines, whose knowledge of our medicinal flora has been strangely correct as since proven."

There are few records of the medicinal use of witch hazel by the Indians of New Brunswick, most likely due to the scarcity of the shrub in this province. It is reported that the Micmacs of Nova Scotia steeped witch hazel twigs, soaked the liquid in a cloth, and inhaled the fumes, apparently as an aphrodisiac and, coincidentally, to relieve headache.

Further west in the Wisconsin — southern Manitoba area several tribes used witch hazel to soothe sore muscles. The Potawatomi steamed the twigs to medicate their sweat baths and the Menomini concocted a liniment by steeping the twigs in boiling water. In eye-witness accounts from 1744 and 1751, white pioneers claimed to have seen near-blindness in Mohawk children cured by applying a lotion made from witch hazel bark.

More than a century later the first factory manufacturing various medicines derived from witch hazel was established in New England. Twigs of wild witch hazel collected in late autumn were distilled with alcohol to form an aqueous extract. Witch hazel extract was bottled and marketed under brand names such as *Pond's*, *Hawe's* and *Dickinson's*. It was recommended for bruises, sprains and skin abrasions. By 1952 the U.S. industry had grown to a production level of over two million litres of extract annually. It has since declined amid competition from a host of new products.

Extract of witch hazel is still available in drug stores today under a variety of brand names. Witch hazel is also a component of some after-shaves, skin cosmetics, eye lotions, ointments, soaps and mouthwashes. Hamamelis water is the primary ingredient in at least one commercial hemorrhoidal preparation.

Witch hazel is the only shrub which flowers in autumn.

water divining . . .

The aura of mystery attached to the witch hazel is further evidenced in its traditional use by water diviners. The diviners cut a forked or Y-shaped branch from a

Curved buds are covered with fine down.

witch hazel shrub, the points of which must have faced north and south as it grew. The branch was held with a prong in each hand, knuckles down and thumbs pointing outward, the long end pointing ahead. When the diviner walked over an underground spring or a deposit or ore, the branch would inexplicaby be tugged downward.

saule *Micmac: elmootjiitjmanagsi*
chaton *Maliseet: kun-oz-os*

WILLOW
(Salix spp.)

Leaf:
All species of willow, both native and exotic, have alternate leaves. They are long, narrow and in most varieties, pointed.

Stem:
Sizes of the various species, varieties and hybrids in New Brunswick range from knee-high dwarf shrubs to rather tall (15 metres) trees such as the black willow. Stems may be single or in clumps. The wood is light and soft but tough. The sapwood is cream-coloured and the heartwood salmon-brown.

Flower:
In May or June flowers of both sexes appear as fuzzy catkins. Male and female flowers are always on separate trees.

Fruit:
Many tiny hairy seeds are released from the female catkins at maturity and are spread by the wind. Willow seeds may begin germination within a matter of hours after landing on the ground.

Twig:
Most willow twigs are slender, smooth and yellowish. The buds, like those of the related poplar, are usually crescent-shaped and pressed close to the twig.

Clump of young willows along a fence row.

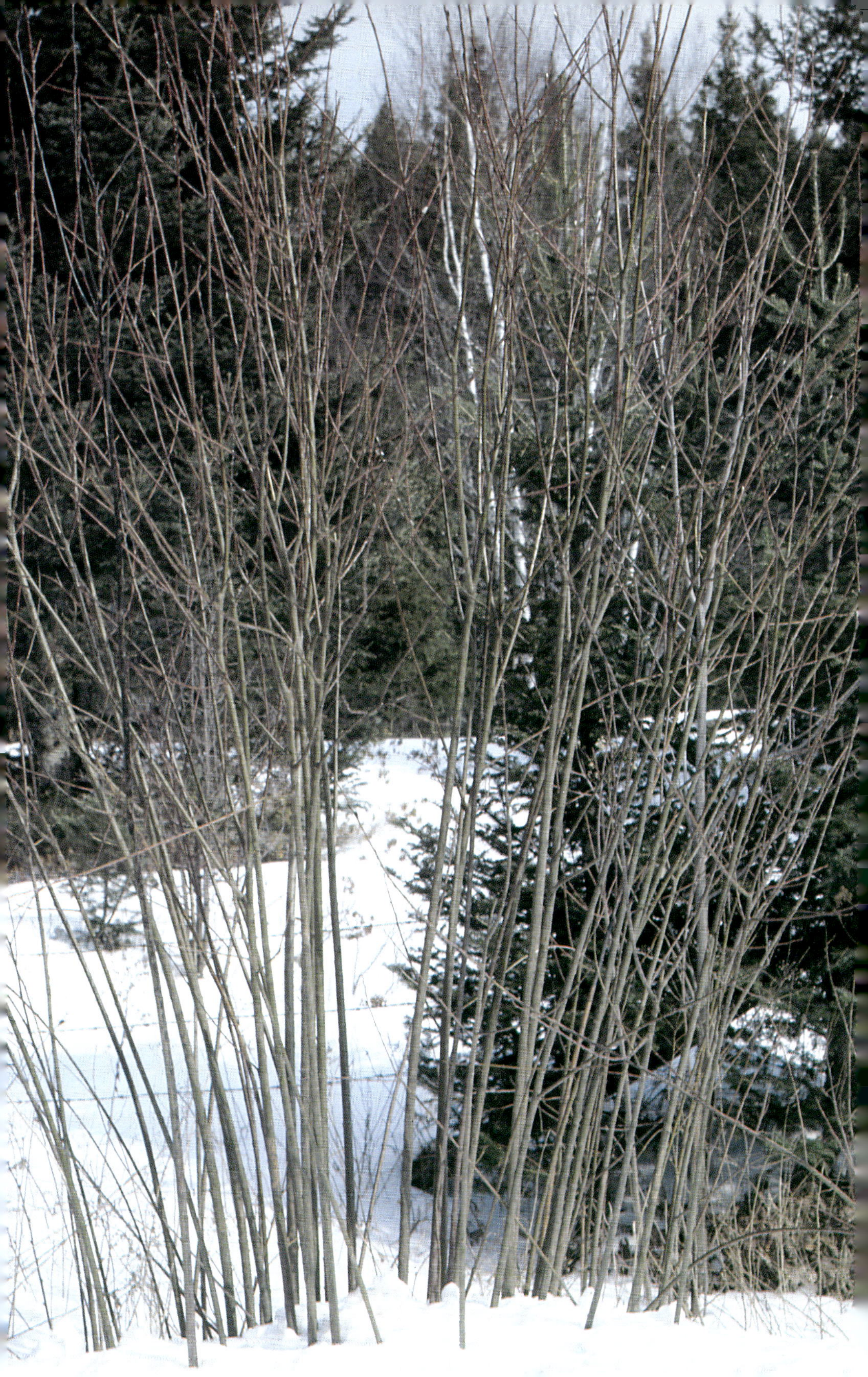

the willows . . .

The word "willow" usually brings two images to mind. The first is the graceful weeping willow, with its long slender limbs drooping to the ground. The other is the pussy willow, whose soft furry silver-grey flowers almost all children have collected.

In New Brunswick there are some twenty-eight species, varieties and natural hybrids of willow, either native to the Atlantic region or introduced from Eurasia. In some cases the species are so similar in appearance that one would need a magnifying glass and a college degree in botany to distinguish the differences.

Possibly the one trait all willows have in common is their ability to

Pussy willows are immature catkins.

Leaves of most willows are long and narrow.

Curved buds are pressed close to the twig.

thrive on wet sites. In the wild, willows are customarily found where there is an abundant supply of water — along streams and river banks, on the edges of bogs, and in low-lying areas with a high water table.

The roots of the weeping willow have been reported to crush city water mains to quench their thirst, and several North American cities have launched campaigns to exterminate willows from city lawns.

Only one native species, the black willow, reaches full tree size in New Brunswick, and it can be found only in scattered areas in the south. The wood of the black willow has been used for lumber, barrels, excelsior and charcoal. All other willows indigenous to this province are small trees or shrubs.

willows and wildlife . . .

Paleontologists, scientists who study fossils, have determined that the willow family of trees and shrubs existed long before the Ice Age. Some seventy million years ago willow leaves were a source of food for several species of dinosaur, including the legendary brontosaurus.

Today the willow is still a favourite of wildlife. Where the shrub abounds willow twigs may comprise a substantial portion of the winter diet of moose. Willow buds are second only to buds of the poplars as preferred food of ruffed grouse (partridge). Beaver, muskrat, red squirrel, deer and snowshoe hare all include willow in their diet. The leaves are rich in both vitamin C and zinc.

as ornamentals . . .

By far the most popular willow planted as an ornamental is the weeping willow, a native of Eurasia, with its characteristic long pendulous limbs. Like the native willows, weeping willow can be propagated simply by cutting a healthy branch about one metre long and planting it in moist ground. The best time is early spring, once the frost has left the ground.

Willows are fast-growing but relatively short-lived shrubs and trees. They are intolerant of shade so must be planted where they will receive full sunlight.

as a medicinal . . .

The documented use of willow bark as a pain reliever dates back to the golden age of the Greek Empire, some 2400 years ago.

Interestingly, at about the same time the native people of North America were prescribing willow bark tea for fever and headache.

The following excerpt from John Gerarde's *Herball* illustrates the state of the art in European medicine late in the sixteenth century:

"The leaves and barke of Willowes do stay the spitting of bloud whatsoever in man or woman, if the said leaves and barke be boiled in wine and drunke. The greene boughes with the leaves may very well be brought into chambers and set about the beds of those that be sicke of fevers, for they do mightily cool the heat of the aire . . ."

Late in the nineteenth century, the active ingredients of willow were isolated and synthesized into acetylsalicylic acid (ASA), and marketed under the name "Aspirin".

Beaver use willow for dam and lodge construction.

Female catkins in late May.

The familiar pussy willows, one of the first signs of spring.

The Indians of New Brunswick found several other uses for willow roots, bark and leaves, both medicinal and otherwise. Micmac medicine men applied poultices of willow bark to heal bruises and stop bleeding. Maliseets would drink a willow tea before meals to stimulate the appetite. Dried willow leaves were often smoked in ceremonial pipes, the stems of which were made of hollowed-out willow twigs.

moosewood   *bois d'orignal*   Micmac: *epgateo-ôôg*
witch-hobble   *viorne à feuilles d'aulne*   Maliseet: *a-dok-im-os*

HOBBLEBUSH
(Viburnum alnifolium)

Leaf:
The opposite leaves are large, round and dark green. The upper surface is textured and the edges are finely toothed. In autumn the leaves turn a deep to reddish purple.

Stem:
The main stem (if there is one main stem) rarely grows beyond three metres high or four to five centimetres in diameter. Bark is smooth and purplish brown. Long horizontal branches weighed down by snow or fallen trees will rest on the ground, send down roots, and a clone of the original shrub will spring up. Botanists call this "layering".

Flower:
From a distance each blossom may appear to be one large showy flower. In fact each blossom consists of an outer circle of sterile white flowers surrounding an inner cluster of small fertile flowers. Blossoms appear in late May and June.

Fruit:
Oblong berries are about 5 mm long and develop in clusters. The berries are green in August, then turn yellow, orange, red and finally purplish-black at maturity in October. If picked just before they drop from the shrub they are quite tasty, but the low ratio of fruit to stone means a lot of gathering for a little bit of eating.

Twig:
Long paddle-shaped, cinnamon-brown buds form at ends of twigs in late summer, a key to identification of this shrub throughout the fall and winter.

Large round leaves develop in pairs.

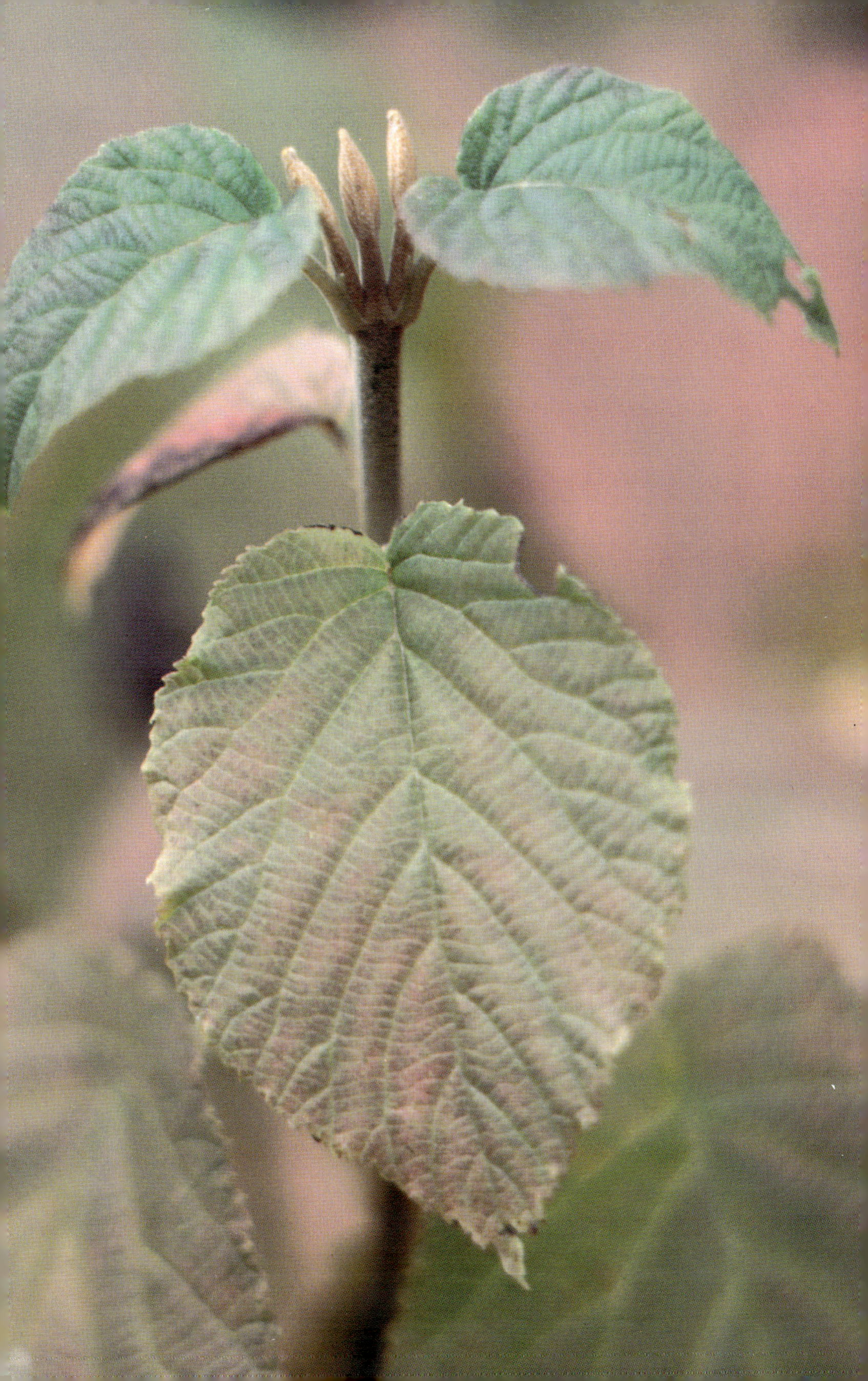

hobblebush...

Hobblebush is one of two shrubs which share the common name "moosewood". The other is striped maple. The two species have several characteristics in common and are frequently found on similar sites, often growing side by side. However, they belong to very different family groups.

Striped maple is a true maple while hobblebush belongs to the honeysuckle family, which includes elderberries, viburnums and of course the honeysuckles. Two other species of viburnums are included in this book — wild raisin and high bush cranberry. All viburnums are tolerant of shade and are usually found growing beneath larger trees, on forest edges and along roadsides. They thrive on moist well-drained soils, which may range from quite acid to slightly alkaline. The presence of hobblebush usually indicates a good site for yellow birch, red spruce and sugar maple.

as an ornamental...

The large white flowers and deep green foliage can be used to best advantage in landscaping shaded corners. Once planted, hobblebush will spread by underground stems (rhizomes) and by layering. Seed is spread when small mammals eat the fruit, but is destroyed in the digestive systems of some birds.

Leaves turn a burgundy red in autumn.

Tiny fertile flowers are surrounded by larger sterile flowers.

To plant hobblebush from seed, gather fruit when red in the fall. Sow in the garden, covering with sawdust as a mulch. Complete germination will not occur until the second summer, at the end of which the seedlings will be ready for transplanting. A snow fence roof above the seedbed will provide the necessary partial shade conditions. A similar technique is often used on balsam fir seedbeds by Christmas tree growers.

wildlife . . .

In the wild, tangled clumps of hobblebush provide safe nesting sites for many songbirds, including warblers. In years when the fruit is plentiful, ruffed grouse, squirrels and chipmunks find it a favourite. In winter the twigs and buds are a particularly valuable source of protein and energy for browsing animals. At a time when food is scarce and survival is difficult, white-tailed deer, moose and snowshoe hares look to hobblebush to bolster their diet.

as a medicinal . . .

Indian medicine men prescribed rubbing of crushed hobblebush leaves on the head of the patient suffering from migraine. The bark, similar in appearance to that of its relative the high bush cranberry, has been substituted for that species and marketed to pharmaceutical companies as "cramp bark". It apparently has the same uterine sedative qualities as the high bush cranberry, but contains an unidentified toxin.

*american
cranberry bush* *viorne trilobée* Micmac: *nipmanagsi*
guelder rose *pimbina* Maliseet: *mi-bi-min-aks*
cramp bark *quatre-saison des bois*

HIGH BUSH CRANBERRY
(Viburnum trilobum)

Leaf:
Leaves are opposite, three-lobed, and generally maple-like in appearance. Leaf edges may be smooth or toothed. Leaf shape may vary considerably, even on the same shrub.

Stem:
Stems are usually forked near the ground, giving the tall (2 - 4 m) shrub a somewhat bushy appearance. The bark is smooth and grey.

Flower:
Oval, flat-topped clusters 10-12 cm across bloom at the ends of branches in late June. Each cluster is composed of tiny yellowish fertile flowers surrounded by showier white sterile blossoms.

Fruit:
After fertilization the sterile flowers wither and disappear and the central flowers evolve into bright red berries. After a few frosts in September they turn glossy or translucent, and are considered ripe. They may hang from the ends of branches throughout the winter. Each juicy berry contains a single flat stone.

Twig:
Pairs of shiny red or greenish-yellow opposite buds develop on smooth grey-brown twigs. The ends of the twigs die back after leaf fall, but may remain attached to the rest of the twig. There is no terminal bud.

Translucent red berries remain well into winter.

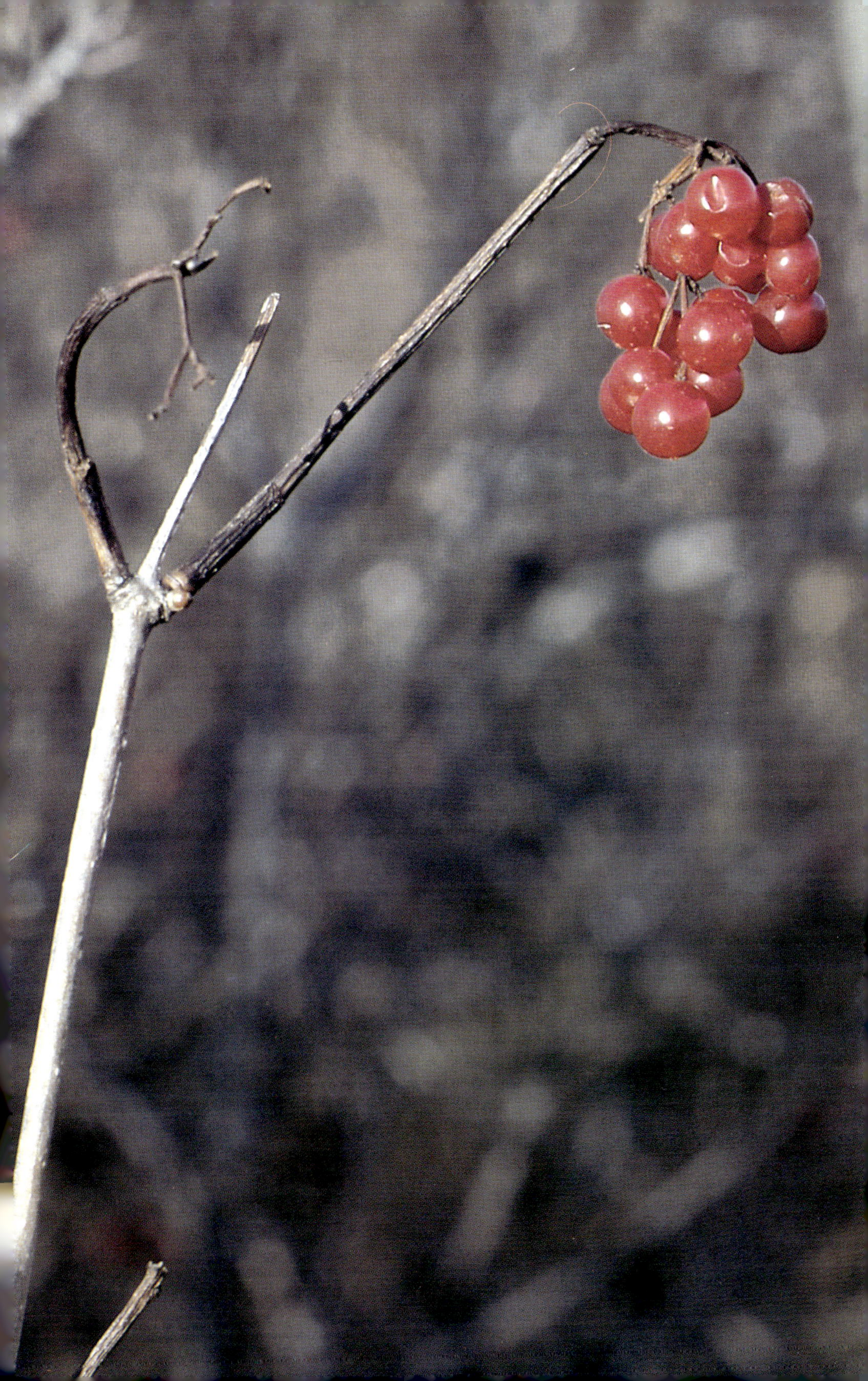

high bush cranberry...

Despite its common name, high bush cranberry is not a true cranberry. It will not be found on the supermarket shelf. But early North American settlers found the fruit so similar in colour, shape, and particularly taste that they dubbed it the "bush cranberry". For all intents and purposes the fruit may be substituted in any recipe calling for cranberries.

High bush cranberry is one of only a few shrubs native to all ten provinces. In New Brunswick it can be found throughout the province, but is somewhat scarce in the eastern counties. The cranberry tree, as it is often called, thrives on rich moist soils, along stream banks and along the edges of damp woods. But it is equally at home on rocky sites like those on the Kingston Peninsula.

as an ornamental...

The high bush cranberry is the country cousin of the popular ornamental Snowball Bush marketed by most commercial nurseries. The Snowball is much showier in blossom, but is sterile and can not bear fruit. For landscaping purposes the two shrubs would complement each other — one producing large showy flowers in summer and the other heavy clusters of scarlet berries throughout the winter.

Clusters of fruit are most attractive in autumn.

wildlife...

A hedge or windbreak of high bush cranberry will provide both food and cover for nesting and roosting birds. The tart berries are rarely first choice among the feathered set, but they can be a crucial emergency food when there is little else available. The fruit is often a prime food source for ruffed grouse in fall and winter. Cedar waxwings and grosbeaks are also attracted by the fruit.

High bush cranberry most commonly reproduces by seed. If a few plants are desired for landscaping, search out small seedlings beneath or near old shrubs. Dig them up and transplant them to their new home. Tilling, or at least removal of the sod before planting, will help ensure survival. Use a nitrogen-rich fertilizer such as urea, ammonium nitrate, or well-rotted manure for the first few years. Cultivation will help as well. The young bushes should begin flowering and fruiting in three to five years.

as a medicinal...

The bark of the high bush cranberry was used for the relief of cramps of various kinds, both in medieval Europe and in North America before the arrival of the white man. Hence the common name "cramp bark". Cramp bark

Leaves of high bush cranberry can be quite variable in shape.

was used as a uterine sedative during pregnancy, to ease the pain of contractions in childbirth, and to relieve menstrual cramps. Early settlers referred to it as "squawbush." It was also said that a tea brewed from the bark would prevent miscarriage.

Both the Maliseets and Micmacs of New Brunswick steeped the berries as a cure for swollen glands and the mumps. The bitter fruit also provided a rare winter source of vitamin C and was eaten to prevent scurvy.

For many years the bark, with its active ingredient "viburnin", was listed as an official drug in the U.S. Pharmacopoeia. At one time the bark was collected and sold to

Ends of twigs die back in autumn.

Tiny fertile flowers are surrounded by large white sterile flowers.

pharmaceutical companies. It was also claimed that the bark was a diuretic, i.e., it would increase urine flow.

high bush cranberry jelly . . .

Cover 1 grape basket of cranberries with water and boil. Strain through jelly bag. Add 1 cup sugar per cup of juice and boil to jelly stage. Skim off foam and put in jars.
Note: High bush cranberries while cooking may smell a little like dirty socks. The final product won't taste that way.

courtesy of
Lucy MacPherson, Kingston

witherod
appalachian tea
false paraguay tea

viorne cassinoide
alisier
poire d'ourse
bourdaine

Micmac: sginaganmosi

WILD RAISIN
(Viburnum cassinoides)

Leaf:
Leaves are opposite and rather thick. Leaf edges vary from smooth to wavy toothed, even on the same plant. They are long (up to 10 cm) and narrow, with pointed tips. In autumn, leaves turn from deep green to pink or crimson.

Stem:
Multiple, long, lithe stems, up to three metres high, form a rounded crown. The bark is greyish-brown and smooth.

Flower:
From the middle to the end of June, umbrella-shaped clusters of creamy-white blossoms appear at the ends of branches. The individual flowers have five petals and have an unpleasant scent.

Fruit:
Clusters of small, oval berries ripen in late August and September, turning pink, then blue-black. Each edible berry contains one large flattened seed. If not consumed early by birds, the fruit tend to shrivel up on the shrub. Hence the name "wild raisin."

Twig:
Distinctive, pointed, cinnamon-brown terminal buds make this shrub easily identifiable in winter. Twigs are slender, light brown, and bear opposite buds.

Ripe berries are bluish-black.

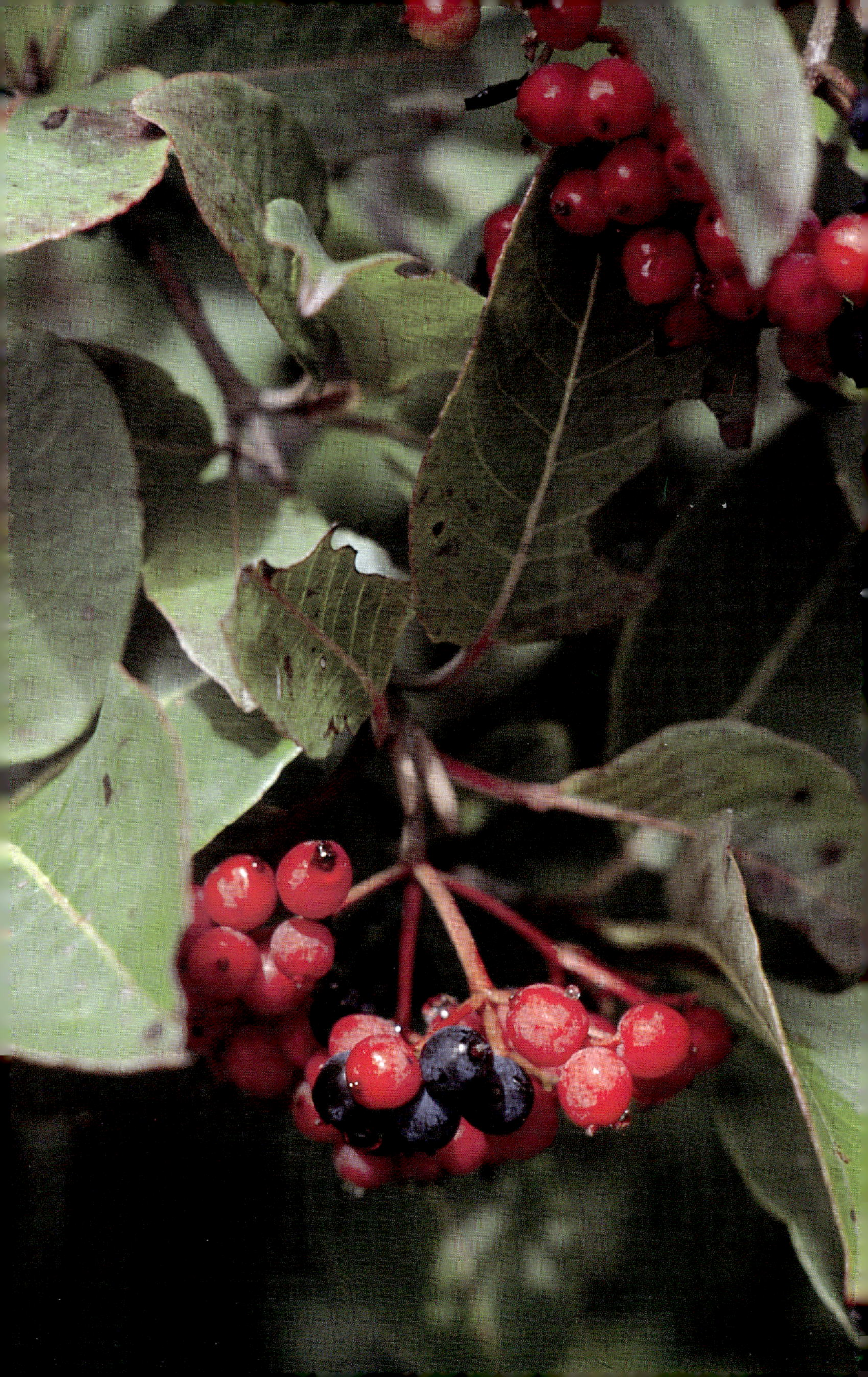

wild raisin...

Viburnum cassinoides, the third and final member of the *Virburnums* described in this book, is the most common of this family, and can be found throughout most of the province. It is very closely related to and resembles the nannyberry, *Viburnum lentago*, which grows in New Brunswick only in the extreme southwest, near the Maine border.

Wild raisin can grow just about anywhere. It may be found on wet acidic soils along the edges of bogs and swamps, or on dry upland sites. It may grow in the shade or in nearly full sunlight. Throughout the province wild raisin lines the sides of country roads. It is also found in low wet wooded areas, on the banks of brooks and along farm fence rows. It is frequently one of the pioneer species which appear after forest fires, along with grey birch, pin cherry, poplar and jack pine.

as an ornamental...

Wild raisin is the perfect native ornamental shrub. Its creamy-white clusters of blossoms in spring, deep green summer foliage, and clusters of bright pink fruit in the fall give the wild raisin aesthetic appeal throughout the warmer months. It is easily cultivated, requires little maintenance, and will withstand extremes of soil, temperature, moisture and shade. It is not

Clusters of creamy-white blossoms appear in June.

prone to damage from insects and diseases.

The simplest method of propagation is by transplanting young seedlings dug up along roadsides. To plant from seed, pick fruit when ripe (the colour of blueberries), air dry, and sow in a prepared seedbed, mulching with sawdust. Seed will not germinate until the second spring after planting. Partial shade provided by erecting a snow fence horizontally over the seedbed will simulate natural growing conditions. Seedlings can be transplanted to their permanent location after the first growing season.

A typical cluster of wild raisin in winter.

Foliage turns pink or crimson in autumn.

wildlife . . .

Wild raisin is a consistent bearer of fruit, providing a regular annual food supply for both birds and mammals. Robins, cedar waxwings and blackbirds migrating south in the fall feast on the abundant berries. Ruffed grouse, snowshoe hares, chipmunks, squirrels, mice and skunks all dine on the fruit. In this way the seed is scattered and new shrubs may spring up. In winter, wild raisin twigs are browsed by white-tailed deer, forming a substantial part of their diet when food is not plentiful. In summer, deer will eat the leaves as well. It has been reported, however, that the leaves contain a cyanide compound and may be **poisonous** to humans, livestock and pets.

As well as being a source of food, wild raisin provides valuable cover for wild mammals and birds, especially along fence rows and forest edges or where it forms small thickets.

as a medicinal . . .

Historically there is little evidence of any part of the wild raisin being used as a medicine, either by native people or the early settlers. The juice of the fruit reportedly has a flavour not unlike that of prune juice and apparently has similar effects.

Immature fruit clusters are pink.

In some years, wild raisin are prolific bearers of fruit.

Quotation Sources . . .

p. 27	Rafinesque, C. S.,	**Medical Flora or Manual of Medical Botany of the United States** Vol II. Samuel C. Atkinson, Philadelphia, 1830. found in: Erichsen-Brown, Charlotte, **Use of Plants for the Past 500 Years.** Breezy Creek Press, Aurora, Ont. 1979.
p. 33	Isham, James	**Observations on Hudson's Bay and Notes on a book entitled 'A Voyage to Hudson Bay in the Dobbs Galley, 1746-7',** E. E. Rich & A.M. Johnson eds., Hudson's Bay Record Soc. Publ. 12, London, 1949. found in: Erichsen-Brown, 1979.
p. 37	Smith, Huron H.,	**Ethnobotany of the Menomini.** Bull. Pub. Mus. Milwaukee 4: 1-82, 1923. found in: Erichsen-Brown, 1979.
p. 45	Hoffman, W. J.,	**The Mide'wiwin or "Grand Medicine Society" of the Ojibway.** 7th Ann. Rep., Bur. of Ethnology, Washington, 1891, p. 200.
p. 49	Mechling, W. H.,	**The Malicete Indians with Notes on the Micmacs.** University of Ottawa, Anthropologica 8: 239-263, 1959. p. 248.
p.55	Fernald, M. L., A. C. Kinsey & R. C. Rollins,	**Edible Wild Plants of Eastern North America.** Harper & Row, New York, 1958, p. 351.
p. 68	Wood, William,	New England prospect, Prince Soc., Boston, 1865. Found in: Erichsen-Brown, 1979.
p. 79	LeClercq, Chrestien,	**New Relations of Gaspesia.** William F. Ganong, trans. & ed., The Champlain Society, Toronto, 1910. p. 297.
p. 89	Millspaugh, Charles F.,	**American Medicinal Plants.** Dover Publ. Inc., New York, 1974. p. 228.
p. 96	Gerarde, John, & Thomas Johnson,	**The Herball or General History of Plants.** (1633) Dover Publ. Inc., New York, 1971. found in: Erichsen-Brown, 1979.

Glossary

Alternate: Leaves and buds arranged on twigs singly, with only one at any point.

Opposite: Leaves and buds arranged on twigs in pairs, on opposite sides of twigs.

Simple Leaf: A leaf consisting of a single blade.

Compound Leaf: A leaf composed of several leaflets attached to a central stalk.

Sapwood: The outer circle of growth rings in a stem, composed of living tissue and usually pale.

Heartwood: The inner circle of rings in a stem, composed of non-living tissue, usually darker in colour.

Pith: The soft centre of a twig or stem.

Lenticels: Small, usually oval embossed spots on the bark of some woody species.

Samara: A winged fruit.

Catkin: An elongated cluster of tiny male or female flowers.

Decoction: A tea made by boiling the substance, usually in a covered pot.

Emetic: A substance which when swallowed induces vomiting.

Lateral: Growing on the side of a twig or branch.

Lobe: A segment of a leaf.

Pioneer: A species, usually intolerant of shade, which invades a site after a disturbance such as fire or clearcutting, and occupies the site for a short period of time.

Rhizome: An underground horizontal stem.

Rotation: Number of years to grow trees to desired size for harvest.

Stolon: A stem which spreads horizontally over the ground and often roots where it touches the ground.

Succession: The long-term orderly process by which plant communities develop, which if not disturbed will ultimately end in a climax forest.

Terminal: Growing at the end of a twig or branch.

Tolerance: Relative ability of a plant to survive in the shade.

Bibliography — Books

Those books marked with an asterisk are recommended reading, and would provide a good basic reference library on the subjects covered in this text.

Anon., **Arbres Indigènes du Canada.** Service Forestier, Ministère des Ressources et du Developpement économique, Ottawa, 1950.

Angier, Bradford, **Field Guide to Edible Wild Plants.** Stackpole Books, Harrisburg, Pa., 1974.

Assiniwi, Bernard, **Survie en Forêt.** Les Editions Leméac Inc., Ottawa, 1972.

Billington, Cecil, **Shrubs of Michigan.** Cranbrook Inst. of Science, Bull. #20, 2nd. ed. Cranbrook Press, Bloomfield Hills, Mich., 1949.

Blakeslee, Albert Francis, & Chester Deacon Jarvis, **Northeastern Trees in Winter.** Dover Publ. Inc., New York, 1972.

Burns, G. P., & C. H. Otis, **The Trees of Vermont.** Vermont Agr. Exp. Sta. Bull #194, 1915.

Chase, Andrew J., Fay Hyland & Harold E. Young, **Puckerbrush Pulping Studies.** Life Sciences & Agric. Exp. Sta., Univ. of Maine, Orono, Tech Bull.# 49, 1971.

Chase, Andrew J., Fay Hyland & Harold E. Young, **The Commercial Use of Puckerbrush Pulp.** Life Sciences & Agric. Exp. Sta., Univ. of Maine, Orono, Tech. Bull. # 65, 1973.

Denys, Nicolas, **The Description and Natural History of the Coasts of North America (Acadia).** Trans. by William F. Ganong. Champlain Society, Toronto, 1908.

*Erichsen-Brown, Charlotte, **Use of Plants for the Past 500 Years.** Breezy Creek Press, Aurora, Ont., 1979.

Fernald, Merritt Lyndon, **Gray's Manual of Botany.** 8th ed. American Book Co., New York, 1950.

*Fernald, M. L., A. C. Kinsey & R. C. Rollins, **Edible Wild Plants of Eastern North America.** Harper & Row, New York, 1958.

*Gill, John D., & William M. Healy, **Shrubs and Vines for Northeastern Wildlife.** USDA For. Ser. Gen. Tech. Rep. NE-9, Upper Darby, Pa., 1974.

Grieve, Mrs. M., **A Modern Herbal (Vol. I & II).** Dover Publ. Inc., New York, 1971.

Grimm, William Carey, **The Book of Shrubs.** Bonanza Books, New York, 1957.

Gunther, Robert T., ed., **The Greek Herbal of Dioscorides.** John Goodyer, trans. Hafner Publ., New York, 1959.

Hedrick, U. P., ed., **Sturtevant's Edible Plants of the World.** Dover Publ. Inc. New York, 1972.

Hinds, Harold, R., **Annotated Checklist of the Woody Plants of New Brunswick.** Can. For. Serv. Inf. Report M-X-103, Dept. of Environment, Fredericton, 1979.

*Hosie, R. C., **Native Trees of Canada.** Can. For. Serv., Dept. of Environment, Ottawa, 1969.

Hylton, William H., ed, **The Rodale Herb Book.** Rodale Press, Emmaus, Pa., 1974.

Krochmal, Arnold, & Connie Krochmal, **A Guide to the Medicinal Plants of the United States.** Quadrangle/NY Times Book Co., New York, 1973.

Krochmal, Arnold, Russel S. Walters & Richard M. Doughty, **A Guide to Medicinal Plants of Appalachia.** USDA Forest Service Agric. Handbook # 400, 1971.

Lacey, Laurie, **Micmac Indian Medicine.** Formac Ltd., Antigonish, N.S., 1976.

Lamoureux, Gisèle et al, **Plantes Sauvages Printanières.** La Documentation Québécoise, Québec, 1975.

Lanthier, Aldéi, **Les Plantes Médicinales Canadiennes.** Editions Paulines, Montréal, 1977.

Laurent, Joseph, **New Familiar Abenakis & English Dialogues.** Leger Brousseau, Québec, 1884.

Le Clercq, Fr. Chrestien, trans. by William F. Ganong, **New Relation of Gaspesia.** The Champlain Society, Toronto, 1910.

Lewis, Walter H., & Memory P. F. Elvin-Lewis, **Medicinal Botany — Plants Affecting Man's Health.** John Wiley & Sons, Toronto, 1977.

Liscinsky, Stephen A., **The Pennsylvania Woodcock Management Study.** Pennsylvania Game Commission Res. Bull. # 171, Harrisburg, Pa., 1972.

Magee, Dennis W., **Freshwater Wetlands.** Univ. of Mass. Press, Amherst, 1981.

*Marie — Victorin, Frère, **Flore Laurentienne.** Les Presses de l'Université de Montréal, Montréal, 1964.

*Martin, Alexander C., Herbert S. Zim, & Arnold L. Nelson, **American Wildlife & Plants — A Guide to Wildlife Food Habits.** Dover Publ. Inc., New York, 1961.

McKell, Cyrus M., James P. Blaisdell, & Joe R. Goodin, **Wildland Shrubs — Their Biology and Utilization.** USDA Gen.Tech. Rep. INT-1, Intermountain Forest & Range Exp. Sta., Ogden, Utah, 1971.

Medsger, Oliver Perry, **Edible Wild Plants.** The Macmillan Co., New York, 1940.

Meyer, Joseph E., **The Herbalist.** Clarence Meyer Publ., 1972.

Millspaugh, Charles F., **American Medicinal Plants.** Dover Publ. Inc., New York,1974.

Ministère des Terres et Forêts, Québec, **Petite Flore Forestière du Québec** Editions France-Amérique, Montréal, 1974.

Muenscher, Walter Conrad, **Poisonous Plants of the United States.** Macmillan Co., New York, 1957.

Munro, Derek, **A Floristic Study of Kouchibouguac National Park.** Biosystematics Research Inst., Ottawa, 1979.

Newhall, Charles S., **The Shrubs of Northeastern America.** G. P. Putnam's Sons, New York, 1897.

Peterson, RogerTory, **A Field Guide to the Birds East of the Rockies.** Houghton Mifflin Co., Boston, 1980.

Rand, Rev. Silas Tertius, **Dictionary of the Language of the Micmac Indians.** Nova Scotia Printing Company, Halifax, 1888.

Rand, Silas T., **A First Reading Book in the Micmac Language.** Nova Scotia Printing Company, Halifax, 1875.

Robson, John R.K., & Joel N. Elias, **The Nutrional Value of Indigenous Wild Plants: An Annotated Bibliography.** Whitson Publ. Co., Troy, NY, 1978.

Saunders, Charles Francis, **Edible and Useful Wild Plants of the United States and Canada.** Dover Publications Inc., New York, 1934.

Schopmeyer, C. S., **Seeds of Woody Plants in the United States.** USDA Agriculture Handbook No. 450, Washington, 1974.

Scoggan, H.J., **The Flora of Canada** (I-IV), Nat. Museum of Natural Sciences No. 7, Nat. Museum of Canada, Ottawa, 1978.

*Soper, James H., Margaret L. Heimburger, **Shrubs of Ontario.** Royal Ontario Museum, Toronto, 1982.

Speck, Frank, G., **Penobscot Man.** Univ. of Pennsylvania Press, Philadelphia, 1940.

Stone, Eric, **Medicine Among the American Indians.** Hafner Publ. Co., New York, 1962.

Tomikel, John, **Edible Wild Plants of Eastern United States and Canada.** Allegheny Press, California, Pa., 1976.

*Turner, Nancy J., & Adam F. Szczawinski, **Edible Wild Fruits and Nuts of Canada.** Nat. Museums of Canada, Ottawa, 1979.

Université de Moncton, **Es-te bâdré de tes vivres? Medecine Traditionelle en Acadie.** Collection Folklore Acadien Vol. I, Centre d'Etudes Acadiennes, University of Moncton, Moncton, 1979.

Van Dersal, William R., **Native Woody Plants of the United States, Their Erosion Control and Wildlife Values.** USDA Misc. Publ, #303, Washington, 1939.

*Vogel, Virgil J., **American Indian Medicine.** Univ. of Oklahoma Press, Norman, Okla., 1970.

Wallis, Wilson D., & Ruth Sawtell Wallis, **The Micmac Indians of Eastern Canada.** Univ. of Minnesota Press, Minneapolis, 1955.

White, James, ed., **Handbook of Indians of Canada.** republished from "Handbook of American Indians North of Mexico" Part I (1907) & Part II (1910), Bureau of American Technology. Appendix to 10th Report, Geographic Board of Canada, Ottawa, 1913, (Coles Canadiana ed.)

Bibliography — Periodicals

Following is a listing of articles appearing in periodicals, scientific journals, Canadian and U.S. government reports, for those who may wish to delve more deeply into the topics covered.

Adney, E. Tappan, **The Malecite Indian's Names for Native Berries and Fruits, and Their Meanings.** Acad. Naturalist. 1 (3): 103-110, 1944.

Anonymous, **Little Journeys to Chemurgic Industries — Witch Hazel.** Chemurgic Digest 2: 193, 1943.

Bedard, J, M. Crête & E. Audy, **Short-term Influence of Moose Upon Woody Plants of an Early Seral Wintering Site in Gaspé Peninsula, Québec.** Can. J. For. Res. 8: 407-415, 1978.

Beauchamp, W.M., **Onondaga Plant Names.** J Amer. Folklore 15: 91-103, 1902.

Berry, Edward, W., **Notes on the History of the Willows and Poplars.** Plant World 20: 16-28, 1917.

Blake, Sidney, F., **On the Names of Some Species of Viburnum.** Rhodora 20: 11-15, 1918.

Bond, G., **Istotopic Studies of Nitrogen Fixation in Non-Legume Root Nodules.** Annals of Botany 21(84): 516-521, 1957.

Boyd, Ivan L., **An Ecological Study of Four Species of Sumac in Relation to Development and Growth on Eroded Soil.** Kans. Acad. Sci. Trans. 47: 51-59, 1943.

Brooks, Harlow, **The Medicine of the American Indian.** Bull. N.Y. Acad. Med. Ser. 2(5): 509-537, 1929.

Brown, Charles, P., **Food of Maine Ruffed Grouse by Seasons and Cover Types.** J. Wildl. Manage. 10 (1): 17-28, 1946.

Burgess, T. J. W., **On the Beneficial and Toxic Effects of the Various Species of Rhus.** Can. Pharm. J. 14 (6): 161-168, 1881.

Carr, Lloyd G., & Carlos Westez, **Surviving Folktales and Herbal Lore Among the Shinnecock Indians of Long Island.** J. Amer. Folklore 58: 117-123, 1945.

Chamberlain, Alexander, F., **Notes and Queries.** J.Amer. Folklore 14: 203, 1901.

Chamberlain, Lucia Sarah, **Plants Used by the Indians of Eastern North America.** Amer. Naturalist 35: 1-10, 1901.

Chamberlain, Montague, **Maliseet Vocabulary.** Harvard Cooperative Society, Cambridge, Mass, 1844.

Chamberlain, Montague, **Indians in New Brunswick in Champlain's Time.** Acadiensis 4: 280-295, 1904.

Chandler, R. Frank, Lois Freeman & Shirley N. Hooper, **Herbal Remedies of the Maritime Indians.** J. Ethnopharmacology 1: 49-68, 1979.

Cheyney, E. G., **The Root System of the Hazel.** J. Forest. 26: 1046-1047, 1928.

Cook, David B., & Frank C. Edminster, **Survival and Growth of Shrubs Planted for Wildlife in New York.** J. Wildl. Manage. 8: 185-191, 1944.

Craig, D. L., **Elderberry Culture in Eastern Canada.** Can. Dept. Agriculture, Publ. #1280, 1966.

Dale, Martin E., **Interplant Alder to Increase Growth in Strip-Mine Plantations.** U.S. Forest Service, Central States Forest Exp. Sta. CS-14, 1963.

Daly, G. T., **Nitrogen Fixation by Nodulated Alnus Rugosa.** Can. J. Bot. 44 (12): 1607-1621, 1966.

Del Tredici, Peter, **Legumes Aren't the Only Nitrogen-Fixers.** Horticulture, March 1980: 30-33.

Delver, P., & A. Post, **Influence of Alder Hedges on the Nitrogen Nutrition of Apple Trees.** Plant and Soil 28(2): 325-336, 1968.

Dyer, Richard F., Andrew J. Chase & Harold E. Young, **Pulp from Presently Non-commercial Woody Perennials.** Pulp and Paper Magazine, January, 1968.

Edminster, Frank C., **Use of Shrubs in Developing Farm Wildlife Habitat.** N. Am. Wild. Conf. Trans. 15:519-550, 1950.

Euler, David, **Vegetation Management for Wildlife in Ontario.** Ont. Min. Nat. Res., 1979.

Evans, Harold J., **Biological Nitrogen Fixation for Food and Fiber Production.** Science 197: 332-339, 1977.

Feller-Demalsy, Marie-José, & Yvan Lamontagne, **Analyse Pollinique des Miels du Québec.** Apidologie 10 (4): 313-340, 1979.

Fernald, M. L., **Eastern North American Representatives of Alnus Incana.** Rhodora 47: 333-361, 995-1000, 1945.

Fulling, Edmund, H., **American Witch Hazel — History, Nomenclature and Modern Utilization.** Econ. Bot. 7: 359-381, 1953.

Grange, Wallace B., & W. L. McAtee, **Improving the Farm Environment for Wildlife.** USDA Farmers' Bull. 1719, 1934.

Hagar, Stansbury, **Micmac Magic and Medicine.** J. Amer. Folklore 9 (34): 170-177, 1896.

Halls, L. K., & R. Alcaniz, **Browse Plants Yield Best in Forest Openings.** J. Wildl. Manage. 32 (1): 185-196, 1968.

Hamilton, W. J. Jr., **Notes on Food of Red Foxes in New York and New England.** J. Mamm. 16: 16-21.

Hamilton, W. J. Jr., **Seasonal Food of Skunks in New York.** J. Mamm. 17: 240-246.

Henkel, Alice, **Wild Medicinal Plants of the U.S.** USDA Bull. #89, 1906.

Henkel, Alice, **American Medicinal Barks.** USDA Bull. #139, 1909.

Henkel, Alice, **American Medicinal Flowers, Fruit and Seeds,** USDA Bull #26, 1913.

Henry, Douglas G., **Foliar Nutrient Concentrations of Some Minnesota Forest Species,** Minn. For. Res. Notes # 241, Univ. of Minn., 1973

Hill, Lewis, **Vintage Elderberries.** Horticulture, June 1983: 44-46.

Hoffman, W. J., **The Midewiwin or "Grand Medicine Society" of the Ojibway.** 7th, Annual Report, Bureau of Ethnology: 198-201, Washington, 1891.

Hoover, Kenneth B., **Hawthorn Studies in Pennsylvania in Relation to Wildlife Values.** Penn. Coop Wildl. Res. Unit Spec. Rep. #5, 1961.

Hosley, N. W., & R. K. Ziebarth, **Some Winter Relations of White-Tailed**

Deer to the Forests in North Central Massachusetts. Ecology 16 (4): 535-553, 1935.

Howard, Charles D., **Prussic Acid in Wild Cherry Leaves.** N.H. Agr. Exp. Sta. Bull. # 56: 113-123, 1898.

Hungerford, Kenneth E., **Evaluating Ruffed Grouse Foods for Habitat Improvement.** N. Am. Wildl. Conf. Trans. 22: 380-395, 1957.

Johnson, W. T., W. A. Sinclair & J. A. Weidhass, **Diseases and Insects of Hawthorns and Their Control.** N.Y. State Coll. Agr. Cornell Ext. Bull. #1172, 1966.

Jones, George Neville, **American Species of Amelanchier.** Illinois Biol. Monographs, University of Illinois Press, 1946.

Jones, Ivor, & E. V. Lynn, **Differences in Species of Taxus.** J. Amer. Pharm. Assoc. 22: 528-531, 1933.

Jones, L. R., & F. V. Rand, **Vermont Shrubs and Woody Vines.** Vermont Agr. Exp. Sta. Bull. #145: 49-199, 1909.

King, Ralph T., **Ruffed Grouse Management.** J. Forest. 35: 523-532, 1937.

Korstian, C. F., **The Indicator Significance of Native Vegetation in Determination of Forest Sites.** Plant World 20: 267-287, 1917.

Krefting, L. W., H. L. Hansen, & M. H. Stenlund, **Stimulating Regrowth of Mountain Maple for Deer Browse by Herbicides, Cutting, and Fire.** J. Wildl. Manage. 20 (4): 434-441, 1956.

Krefting, L. W., M. H. Stenlund & R. K. Seemel, **Effect of Simulated and Natural Deer Browsing on Mountain Maple.** J. Wildl. Manage. 30 (3): 481-489. 1966.

Krochmal, Arnold, **Medicinal Plants and Appalachia.** Econ. Bot. 22 (4): 332-337, 1968.

Krochmal, Arnold, **A Guide to Medicinal Plants of Appalachia.** USDA Agric. Handbook 400, 1971.

Lamb, George N., **Willows: Their Growth, Use and Importance.** USDA Bull. #316, 1915.

Liscinsky, Stephen A., **Alder Management.** Woodcock-Grouse Symposium, Newcomb, N. Y., 1973.

Little, E. L. Jr., **Layering After a Heavy Snow Storm in Maryland.** Ecology 25: 112-113, 1944.

Longnecker, G. Wm., & Robert Ellarson, **Landscape Plants that Attract Birds.** Univ. Wisc. Ext. Serv. Circ. #514, 1960.

Lowry, G. L., F. C. Brokow & C. H. J. Breeding, **Alder for Reforesting Coal Spoils in Ohio.** J. Forest. 60: 196-199, 1962.

McAtee, W. L., **How to Attract Birds in Northeastern United States.** USDA Farmers' Bull. #621, 1914.

McDermott, R. E., **Effects of Saturated Soil on Seedling Growth of Some Bottomland Species.** Ecology 35: 36-41, 1954.

McDermott, R. E., **Light as a Factor in the Germination of Some Bottomland Hardwood Seeds.** Jour. Forest. 51: 203-204, 1952.

McKay, Sheila Mary, **A Biosystematic Study of the Genus Amelanchier in**

Ontario. M. Sc. Thesis, Univ. of Toronto, 1973.

Mechling, W. H., **The Malecite Indians with Notes on the Micmacs.** Anthropologica 8: 239-263, 1959.

Morrell, Jennie M. H., **Some Maine Plants and Their Uses — "Wise and Otherwise".** Rhodora 3: 129-132, 1901.

Morton, Julia F., **Principal Wild Food Plants of the United States.** Econ. Bot. 17: 319-330, 1963.

Palmer, Edward, **Food Products of the North American Indians.** USDA Agric. Report # 1871: 404-428.

Park, Barry C., **The Yield and Persistence of Wildlife Food Plants.** J. Wildl. Manage. 6 (2): 118-121, 1942.

Pease, James L., R. H. Vowles & L. B. Keith, **Interaction of Snowshoe Hares and Woody Vegetation.** J. Wildl. Manage. 43 (1): 43-60, 1979.

Post, L. J., **Vegetative Reproduction of Mountain Maple.** Can. Dept. of Forestry Publ. # 1097, 1965.

Post, L. J., **Vegetative Reproduction and the Control of Mountain Maple.** Pulp and Paper Mag. of Can., Oct 17, 1969.

Ruffner, Joseph D., **Plant Performance on Surface Coal Mine Spoil in Eastern United States.** USDA Soil Conservation Service SCS-TP-155, 1978.

Schultes, Richard Evans, **The Widening Panorama in Medical Botany.** Rhodora 65: 97-120, 1963.

Seigler, David, S., **Plants of the Northeastern United States that Produce Cyanogenic Compounds.** Econ. Bot. 30: 395-407, 1975.

Sievers, A. F., **American Medicinal Plants of Commercial Importance.** USDA Misc. Publ. # 77, 1930.

Skinner, Wallace R., **Spring, Summer and Fall Foods of the White-tailed Deer in Central and Southern New Brunswick.** M.Sc. Thesis (Biol.), Univ. of New Brunswick, 1968.

Skutch, A. F., **Early Stages of Plant Succession Following Forest Fires.** Ecology 10: 177-184, 535-537, 1929.

Smithberg, Margaret H., & Conrad J. Weiser, **Patterns of Variation Among Climatic Races of Red Osier Dogwood.** Ecology 49 (3): 495-505, 1968.

Speck, Frank G., **Medicine Practices of the Northeastern Algonquians.** Proc. XIX Intl. Cong. Americanists: 303-321, Washington, 1915.

Speck, Frank G., & Ralph W. Dexter, **Utilization of Animals and Plants by Malecites of New Brunswick.** J. Wash. Acad. Sci. 42 (1): 1-17, 1952.

Speck, Frank G., & Ralph W. Dexter, **Utilization of Animals and Plants by the Micmac Indians of New Brunswick.** J. Wash. Acad. Sci. 41 (8): 250-259, 1951.

Spinner, George P., & James S. Bishop, **Chemical Analysis of Some Wildlife Foods in Connecticut.** J. Wildl. Manage. 14: 175-180, 1950.

Stepka, W., & A. D. Winters, **A Survey of the Genus Crataegus for Hypotensive Activity.** Lloydia 36 (4): 436, 1973.

Tantaquidgeon, Gladys, **Notes on the Origin and Uses of Plants of the Lake St. John Montagnais.** J. Amer. Folklore 45: 265-266, 1932.

Tappeiner, John C., & Hugo H. John, **Biomass and Nutrient Content of Hazel Undergrowth.** Ecology 54 (6): 1342-1348, 1973.

Tappeiner, John C., & A. A. Alm, **Effect of Hazel on the Nutrient Composition of Annual Litter and Forest Floor in Jack and Red Pine Stands.** Minn. For. Res. Notes # 235, April, 1972.

Tarrant, Robert F., & James M. Trappe, **The Role of Alnus in Improving the Forest Environment.** Plant and Soil, Spec. Vol: 335-348, 1971.

Treichler, R., R. W. Stow, & A. L. Nelson, **Nutrient Content of Some Winter Foods of Ruffed Grouse.** J. Wildl. Manage. 10 (1): 12-17, 1946.

Van Camp, John C. Jr., **The Nutrient Element Content of the Foliage of Certain Species of Minor Forest Vegetation.** J. Forest 46: 823-826, 1948.

Van Wart, Arthur F., **The Indians of the Maritime Provinces, Their Diseases and Native Cures.** Can Med Assoc. J. 59: 573-577, 1948.

Veitch, F. P., J. S. Rogers, & R. W. Frey, **American Sumac: A Valuable Tanning Material and Dyestuff.** USDA Bull. # 706, 1918.

Vogel, Virgil J., **American Indian Influence on the American Pharmacopeia.** Am. Ind. Culture & Research Jour. 2(1): 3-7, 1977.

Wainio, Walter W., & E. B. Forbes, **The Chemical Composition of Forest Fruit and Nuts in Pennsylvania.** J. Agr. Res. 62 (10): 627-635, 1941.

Wallis, Wilson D., **Medicines Used by Micmac Indians.** Am. Anthrop. 24: 24-30, 1922.

Wallis, Wilson D., & Ruth Sawtell Wallis, **The Malecete Indians of New Brunswick.** Nat. Mus. Can. Bull. # 148. Anthrop. Ser. # 40, 1957.

Waugh, F. W., **Wild Plants as Food.** Ottawa Naturalist 32: 2-5, 1918.

Waugh, F. W., **Iroquois Foods and Food Preparation.** Can. Dept. Mines Mem. # 86, Anthrop. Ser. # 12, 1916.

Wiegand, K. M., **The Genus Amelanchier in Eastern North America.** Rhodora 14: 117-161, 1912.

Wiegand, K. M., **Additional Notes on Amelanchier.** Rhodora 22: 146-151, 1920.

Wight, W. F., **Native American Species of Prunus.** USDA Bull. # 179, 1915.

Wilde, S. A., **Soil Fertility Standards for Game Food Plants.** J. Wildl Manage. 10 (2): 77-81, 1946.

Yanofsky, Elias, **Food Plants of the North American Indians.** USDA Misc. Publ. # 237, 1936.

Youngken, Heber W., **History, Botany and Pharmacognosy of Viburnum Opulus L. Var. Americanum (Miller) Ait.** J. Am. Pharm. Assoc. 21 (5): 444-462, 1932.

Youngken, Heber, W., **The Drugs of the Northern American Indian** Am. J. Pharm. 96: 485-502, 1924.

Youngken, Heber W., **The Drugs of the Northern American Indian (II).** Am. J. Pharm. 97: 158-185, 257-271, 1925.

Youngken, Heber W., & James C. Munch, **The Pharmacognosy and Pharmacology of Viburnum Alnifolium.** J. Am. Pharm. Assoc. 29: 439-447, 1940.

Notes

Notes

Notes